GREAT NORTHERN RAILWAY GALLERY

A PICTORIAL JOURNEY THROUGH TIME

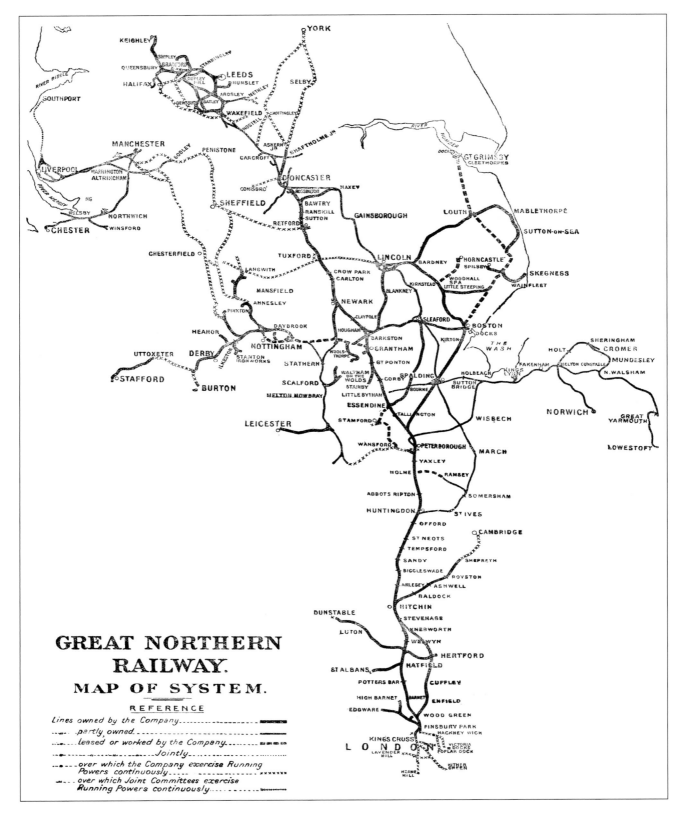

GREAT NORTHERN RAILWAY.

MAP OF SYSTEM.

REFERENCE

Lines owned by the Company	▬▬▬
partly owned	▬ ▬ ▬
leased or worked by the Company	▬ ▬ ▬
Jointly	▬·▬·▬
over which the Company exercise Running Powers continuously	××××××
over which Joint Committees exercise Running Powers continuously	▬▬▬▬▬

Front Cover: 'Atlantic' no.1439, built at Doncaster Works in 1908, departing from Peterborough for London, King's Cross shortly before the outbreak of the First World War. (Detail from a commercial postcard/Author's collection)

Back Cover, top: Stirling '8ft single' no.1007 double-heading the 'Special Scotch Express' with another of the same class at Holloway just north of King's Cross sometime between 1895 and 1900. (Author's collection)

Back Cover, bottom: King's Cross platform 5 with the 1.40pm Leeds express waiting to depart behind 'Atlantic' no. 1400. (H. Gordon Tidey/Author's collection)

GREAT NORTHERN RAILWAY GALLERY

A PICTORIAL JOURNEY THROUGH TIME

MICHAEL A VANNS

PEN & SWORD
TRANSPORT

AN IMPRINT OF PEN & SWORD BOOKS LTD.
YORKSHIRE - PHILADELPHIA

First published in Great Britain in 2019 by
Pen and Sword Transport
An imprint of
Pen & Sword Books Ltd
Yorkshire - Philadelphia

ISBN 978 1 47388 207 2

Typeset by Aura Technology and Software Services, India
Printed and bound in India by Replika Press Pvt. Ltd.

Pen & Sword Books Ltd incorporates the Imprints of Pen & Sword Books Archaeology, Atlas, Aviation,
Battleground, Discovery, Family History, History, Maritime, Military, Naval, Politics, Railways, Select,
Transport, True Crime, Fiction, Frontline Books, Leo Cooper, Praetorian Press, Seaforth Publishing,
Wharncliffe and White Owl.

For a complete list of Pen & Sword titles please contact

PEN & SWORD BOOKS LIMITED
47 Church Street, Barnsley, South Yorkshire, S70 2AS, England
E-mail: enquiries@pen-and-sword.co.uk
Website: www.pen-and-sword.co.uk

or

PEN AND SWORD BOOKS
1950 Lawrence Rd, Havertown, PA 19083, USA
E-mail: Uspen-and-sword@casematepublishers.com
Website: www.penandswordbooks.com

CONTENTS

ACKNOWLEDGMENTS

For reading and commenting on the author's initial text, thanks go to Allan Sibley and Michael Perrins of the Great Northern Railway Society, and for trawling through that society's photograph collection the author is grateful to Paul Craig.

The railway network in Great Britain was created by private companies often in fierce competition with each other. As Derby had been the centre of the Midland Railway empire since 1844, the Great Northern Railway was keen to make its mark on the town when it drove through its Derbyshire & Staffordshire Extension line thirty years later. The highly decorated cast-iron bridge over Derby's Friar Gate made by the local firm of Handyside & Co. and seen here in this Edwardian postcard was certainly made to impress. (Commercial postcard/ Author's collection)

INTRODUCTION

The Great Northern Railway (GNR) was created by an Act of Parliament in 1846 and remained an independent company until absorbed into the London & North Eastern Railway (LNER) in 1923. It ran trains between London and York, into the Eastern Counties and the East Midlands, the West Riding of Yorkshire, into Lancashire and even south of the Thames. Its main line from the terminus at King's Cross, London to just north of Doncaster, formed part of the East Coast route to Scotland. Based on track mileage, both owned by the company and operated jointly with other companies, it ran the fifth most extensive network in Britain after the Great Western Railway

(GWR), Midland Railway (MR), London & North Western Railway (LNWR) and North Eastern Railway (NER). By 1923 it had a fleet of nearly 1,400 locomotives compared with almost 3,300 owned by the LNWR. In terms of net receipts, it ranked as the sixth most profitable railway after those named above with the addition of the Lancashire & Yorkshire Railway (L&YR). It was a good, solid and unpretentious business with a reputation for running fast, punctual and safe trains for both passengers and freight.

With the aid of familiar and not so familiar photographs, the chapters that follow tell the story of its independent years.

Running repairs at King's Cross 'Top Shed'. The site was so named because it was at a higher level than the area just to the west of King's Cross train shed, where there was also a small locomotive facility. No. 299 was put to work in May 1905, one of H.A. Ivatt's 'Atlantics.' (E. Pouteau/ Author's collection)

PREFACE

This book is neither a new or full history of the Great Northern Railway (GNR) but rather an illustrated introduction. The story is a complex one that has been told before in various ways. It was first chronicled from a management perspective by Charles Grinling in his *The History of the Great Northern Railway 1845–1895* (Methuen & Co, 1898). He updated his text in 1903 but the company still had twenty years of independence left. Fifty-five years later, O.S. Nock, with the benefit of hindsight and the advantage of personal experience of steam locomotive operation over a very little altered GNR main line, produced a very readable account that this author still recommends. Extra chapters were added to Grinling's work in 1966, and then in the following decade, John Wrottesley assembled as many facts as he could find about the company and wove them into a three volume work published by B.T. Batsford

between 1979 and 1981. Over the years there have also been a number of books that have concentrated on specific aspects of the company's operations, most of which have been referred to in the creation of this text.

This author's connection with the GNR can be traced back to his great grandfather who worked for the company. He also experienced the dying days of traditional semaphore signalling on the GNR main line and consequently absorbed a little of the atmosphere of the old company that had invested in the equipment over a hundred years earlier. As it must be for many enthusiasts of long vanished railway companies, it was the pre-1920s photographs that fuelled his interest and ultimately led to this book. He hopes it will inspire others to delve further into the history of the Great Northern Railway.

Stoke Prior
August 2018

PLANNING

The railway examined in this book was one of hundreds promoted during what became known as the 'Railway Mania'. In that brief period from 1844 to 1846, millions of pounds were invested in railway schemes both sound and speculative. In November 1844 a project called the 'London & York' was seeking backers for 327.5 miles (527.5km) of railway. It was the main contender in a battle between a number of schemes to build a new railway to connect the capital with York. For many observers the whole project was unrealistic if not fanciful, especially as it had absorbed a number of other projects to form one of the largest railway undertakings yet put before Parliament. Nevertheless, over the next twenty months it fought off sustained opposition, merged with its main rival – the 'Direct Northern' – and in June 1846 gained the Royal Assent for an Act of Parliament under the title the 'Great Northern Railway' (GNR).

The plans

That Act granted the company powers to raise the huge amounts of capital needed to acquire land, alter the alignment of roads, bridge rivers and canals, construct embankments, cuttings, bridges, viaducts, tunnels, lay track, build stations and run trains. The company's intention was to construct two routes roughly in the form of a large capital 'P'. The base of the 'P' was to be located at King's Cross, London and the main stem of the letter was to be the main line to York. This would create the railway equivalent of the Great North Road, passing through many of the well-established coaching towns on that ancient highway. The loop of the 'P' was to curve eastwards out of Peterborough, through Boston, to curve back north-westwards through Lincoln to Bawtry. This was called, appropriately, the 'Loop', with the remainder of the main line from Peterborough, through Grantham, Newark and Retford to Bawtry termed the 'Towns' line.

The main opponent of the scheme had been George Hudson of York, who was the most influential railway promoter and manager of the period. He had worked hard to defend the primacy of the existing railway route between London Euston and York via Birmingham and Derby. In 1844 he had created the Midland Railway (MR) by an amalgamation of the three independent companies that ran the central section of that route. As the first chairman of the MR he championed the construction of eastern branches from Nottingham to Lincoln, via Newark, from Leicester (Syston) to Peterborough, and from Swinton to Doncaster, Gainsborough and Lincoln. His aim was to serve the towns to be reached by the GNR before that railway was built. In 1845 he also became Chairman of the Eastern Counties Railway (ECR) that had been attempting to extend from its existing line out of London, through Cambridge and Lincoln to York. He encouraged that company and the MR to extend out to Boston, Spalding and March where they could make connections. At the end of 1845 he had secured Acts for the MR's extensions to Lincoln and Peterborough and these lines were built and did reach those towns ahead of the GNR. His other plans were not successful and by then the battle to prevent authorisation of the new London to York main line was lost. A suggested amalgamation between his ECR and the rival was soundly rejected by the latter.

Access to the West Riding

The GNR had plans for branch lines to Wakefield and Sheffield but both had been rejected Parliament favouring the Sheffield & Lincolnshire Junction Railway's proposal for a line between Sheffield and Grimsby via Retford and Gainsborough, soon to form part of the Manchester, Sheffield & Lincolnshire Railway's (MS&LR) main line. The GNR then presented a new scheme for a line to Leeds via Wakefield for the Parliamentary Session of 1846. At the same time an independently promoted scheme for a railway between Doncaster and Barnsley – the 'South Yorkshire' (SYR) – was put forward, supported by GNR Deputy Chairman Denison and Baxter, the company's solicitor. Both these projects failed to secure their Acts but an agreement with the Wakefield & Goole Railway (W&GR) immediately compensated for the GNR's failure. In the same Parliamentary session this company gained powers to build two new routes from Pontefract on its recently completed line, one to join the MR at Methley and the other to make an end-on junction with the GNR at Askern

just north of Doncaster. The following year the W&GR amalgamated with the Manchester & Leeds Railway (M&LR) to become the Lancashire & Yorkshire Railway (L&YR). For its support of the Methley and Askern lines the GNR gained running powers over them, and keen to ensure that the company would not deposit another Bill for an independent line to Leeds, Hudson agreed to allow the GNR running powers over the MR between Methley and Leeds. Once there, the GNR decided not to seek to use the MR's station, but to join forces with the L&YR, the Leeds & Thirsk Railway and the London & North Western Railway (LNWR) in building and operating a 'central' station.

The SYR Act was secured in 1847, and the relationship between this railway and the GNR was destined to prove a challenging one over the next twenty years (see p. 32).

Changes of plan

Bawtry was to have been both the place where the 'Loop' and 'Towns' lines met and the junction of the Sheffield branch.

Bawtry station, the two storey buildings seen here designed by Henry Goddard of Lincoln and dating from when the main line opened in 1852. The signalbox was brought into use at the end of 1875 and the single storey shelters some years later. (Commercial postcard/Author's collection)

As the powers to build the latter had not been secured, GNR management had second thoughts about this location and ideas turned to a connection further north at Rossington. For this change of plan a Deviation Bill had to be submitted to Parliament. The inevitable delay to building work this would cause was thought to be worth the alteration but the plans were rejected in both the 1847 and 1848 Parliamentary sessions. The GNR, therefore, came to an accommodation with the MS&LR to use the line it had secured powers to construct from Saxilby (just north-west of Lincoln) to Retford, where a junction was already planned with the GNR main line.

At this time the company was having difficulties raising the necessary finances to fund construction of both the main line between London and Peterborough and the 'Loop'. One of the unexpected consequences of this was a pragmatic agreement with Hudson that allowed the GNR to postpone the building of its own line to York. As noted above, the GNR had gained powers to run over the L&YR from Askern Junction to Wakefield and Leeds. From the L&YR's line at Knottingley, the Y&NMR had secured powers to build a link to Burton Salmon and so the GNR saw the logic of asking Hudson for powers to run over this new link to gain access to York. Perhaps Hudson was aware of the imminent exposure of his financial irregularities because at the beginning of 1849 the GNR got his agreement, probably the last one he signed off before his fall from grace and influence that April.

Gainsborough Lea Road station. The postcard from which this image is taken was posted in August 1910 to a friend in South Harrow from 'aunt Kate', who lived at the two storey station house seen here. (WHS Kingsway Real Photo Series/Author's collection)

The Burton Salmon and Knottingley line was opened in 1850, and content with this connection and another provided by the North Eastern Railway (NER) twenty-one years later, the GNR never resurrected its plans to build an independent line into York. The connection between the 'Loop' and 'Towns' lines, however, remained an unresolved irritant until the end of the 1860s. In September 1849 the MS&LR opened its line between Saxilby (Sykes Junction) and Leverton just east of Retford, which then enabled the GNR to run trains the complete length of its 'Loop' line. This arrangement was never considered to be permanent although it lasted for eighteen years. It was not until 1864 that the GNR finally secured an Act to form its own northern connection between its 'Loop' and 'Towns' lines. The Act included powers to build a bridge over the River Trent at Gainsborough, but as the GNR and MS&LR lines joined there where the latter company already crossed the river, an agreement was reached between the two companies two years later whereby the GNR could use the existing bridge. Branching off the MS&LR line on the west bank of the river and then rejoining the GNR main line at Black Carr Junction, Doncaster, the GNR's final link in its north–south routes opened on 15 July 1867. On the same day, the GNR also brought into use its own station in Gainsborough on Lea Road having run its trains to and from the MS&LR's station in the town since 1849.

Arksey station looking north towards Askern Junction two miles (3.2km) away where, in the summer of 1848, the GNR made its connection with the L&YR. (Commercial postcard/Author's collection)

BUILDING THE MAIN LINE AND LOOP

Almost exactly three years after the passing of the GNR Act for its grand new and direct line between London and York, the company had indeed created a new route between the capital and Yorkshire, but it was one that would have amused George Hudson and troubled GNR shareholders. A passenger could catch a train at the London terminus of the ECR, meander through Lincolnshire and finally end up either in Wakefield or an unfinished station in Leeds. On this new route there were only two sections of new and purely GNR line, one between Werrington Junction, north of Peterborough, through Spalding, Boston and Lincoln to a junction with the MS&LR at Saxilby, and the other between Retford and a junction with the L&YR at Askern.

That the GNR, three years after winning its hard fought Parliamentary battle, was not able to run trains over its own tracks between London and York was an indication of the reaction against railway promotion that had set in following the Mania. Speculation in new lines with a view to quick profits had given way to a curtailment in financial support from a diminished group of now cautious investors. Thomas Brassey, one of the foremost railway contractors of the period, had won the contract to build the main line between London and Peterborough in November 1846, and in January the following year Peto & Betts, another well respected civil engineering firm, had been awarded the contract for the 'Loop' line between Peterborough and Gainsborough. But as the financial squeeze took hold in 1847, management

had been forced to concentrate on its Lincolnshire lines, with the pace of work on Brassey's contract deliberately slowed. In addition, William Cubitt (who had been responsible for drawing up the final plans of the GNR and had been appointed as the company's consulting engineer) had suggested a number of route modifications on the remainder of the main line and 'Loop', and because these had to be submitted for Parliamentary scrutiny as Deviations Bills, this had further delayed construction. It was in this period of uncertainty that the agreement with the Y&NMR already referred to in the previous chapter was entered into, allowing the GNR to rethink it plans for the Doncaster–York section of main line. There was even a suggestion that the route between London and Peterborough should be abandoned altogether and negotiations entered into with the ECR to use its existing line between those two places.

The East Lincolnshire Railway

With a touch of irony the first stretch of line to be operated by the GNR had not been promoted nor was it owned by the company. The East Lincolnshire Railway (ELR) was leased by the GNR and on 1 March 1848, a stretch of this line opened between Grimsby and Louth on the same day as the MS&LR's line between Grimsby and New Holland. The two companies shared the operation of trains on the new route. Six months later services were extended southwards to Firsby, and then on 2 October trains were able to reach Boston and make use of a temporary station there provided by the GNR.

Lincoln station. The platform canopies supported on cast-iron columns with decorative horizontal beams were a feature of a number of stations built in the 1840s. In this detail from an Edwardian postcard the station's resident shunting horse is seen alongside one of the numerous 'through carriages' provided by the GNR. (WHS Kingsway Real Photo Series/Author's collection)

The 'Loop'

A fortnight later the first section of pure GNR line was completed and on 17 October 1848 trains began to run between Peterborough and Lincoln. At Peterborough the GNR had been able to negotiate temporary use of the ECR's station; trains ran from there three miles (4.8km) over the MR's Leicester (Syston) & Peterborough branch as far as Werrington Junction before branching off in a continuous straight line through Spalding to Boston. From Boston the route northwards ran along the banks of the Witham Navigation, twisting its way to Lincoln.

On 18 December 1848, MS&LR trains began operating between Wrawby

Junction (Barnetby) just west of Grimsby and the MR's station in Lincoln, opened two years earlier. At Pelham Street, Lincoln the MS&LR tracks crossed those of the GNR on the level to make an end-on junction with the MR. Given the co-operation between the GNR and MS&LR in this period it was not long before a junction at Pelham Street was formed so that MS&LR trains could be diverted into the GNR's station.

From Lincoln, construction of the GNR westwards to Gainsborough was completed for an opening on 9 April 1849. There the company made another connection with the MS&LR that had just opened the section of its main line between Wrawby Junction and Gainsborough

only seven days earlier. (A continuation of its main line from Gainsborough, through Retford to Woodhouse, on the outskirts of Sheffield, opened on 16 July.) As mentioned in the last chapter, at Gainsborough the GNR shared the MS&LR's station for the next eighteen years despite the awkward reversal involved as the junction had been arranged in anticipation of the GNR continuing west over the River Trent.

The main line

As the GNR's Werrington Junction–Lincoln section of the 'Loop' line was nearing completion, a modest section of the company's main line was edging towards Doncaster. From the junction with the L&YR at Askern, the line southwards to what was to become Arksey station opened in June 1848, and the line extended to a temporary station in Doncaster in

August (some sources say September). The following year the GNR extended south from Doncaster to a junction with the MS&LR at Retford, opening this new line on 4 September 1849. This then created the London–Yorkshire route referred to at the opening of this chapter.

By then work had restarted on the London–Peterborough main line except for the tunnel under Regent's Canal to the site of the London terminus at King's Cross. This had to be postponed because of difficult negotiations with the owners of the hospital on the site that would have to be demolished. Consequently, management had decided to erect a temporary London terminus just north of the tunnel at Maiden Lane where the goods facilities were to be developed. The line was completed in the summer of 1850 and on 5 August that year GNR directors made a special trip northwards

Lincoln's Pelham Street level crossing and Durham Ox Junction looking east. The GNR's tracks to and from Lincoln (Central) station are in the foreground. Curving away to the left is the link to the MS&LR route from Barnetby (Wrawby Junction), while the MR's station (St Mark's) and Newark–Nottingham route is on the right. In the distance are the junctions for Boston, Sleaford and Honington Junction. (Author's collection)

Doncaster station. This arrangement of platform canopies extending over the tracks had originally been intended to protect passengers travelling in carriages without roofs, but by the time the GNR stations were built in this form, the Regulation of Railways Act of 1844 had obliged all companies to provide covered carriages for all passengers. (WHS Kingsway Real Photo Series/Author's collection)

Digswell or Welwyn Viaduct, designed by William and Joseph Cubitt to take the GNR main line across the valley of the River Mimram immediately south of Welwyn (North) station. Constructed of brick, it has forty arches, is approximately 520 yards (475.5m) long and at its highest is about 100ft (30.5m) above the valley. (Commercial postcard/ Author's collection)

The south end of Welwyn South Tunnel, originally named Digswell Tunnel. The north portal of this tunnel and the south portal of Welwyn North Tunnel (Harmer Green) were identical except for the shield seen here, obviously added because the tunnel mouth was visible from the station. All three portals, however, had a central stone tablet into which was carved the date – 1850. (Commercial postcard/ Author's collection)

The majority of original GNR main line stations were simple affairs with low platforms, as this detail from a photograph of Hitchin station taken about 1870 shows. Waiting rooms and lavatories were provided and at town stations refreshment rooms as well, but it was a few more years before the characteristic heavy platform canopies began to appear. (Author's collection)

Apart from the signalbox in the right background opened in 1876, this photograph of Holme station between Huntingdon and Peterborough shows it in original condition. The two storey station master's house has the look of a Turnpike toll house of an earlier generation. (T.W. Latchmore, Hitchin/ Author's collection)

When Henry Goddard was designing the passenger station buildings for the GNR in the late 1840s, the style he chose was termed 'Italianate', characterised by shallow-pitched roofs and windows with semi-circular arch tops. All those features are apparent in the design of Peterborough station, the tower in particular given the appearance of a squat, Italian campanile. (WHS Kingsway Real Photo Series/Author's collection)

from Maiden Lane passing through the new passenger stations at Hornsey, Colney Hatch (later New Southgate), Barnet (later New Barnet), Potters Bar, Hatfield, Welwyn, Stevenage, Hitchin, Arlesey, Biggleswade, Sandy, St Neots, Offord, Huntingdon and Holme to Peterborough. Two days later a public service started and the first through GNR train between London and York ran the following day – 8 August. From the beginning of September 1850 it was possible to travel to Edinburgh from Maiden Lane in twelve hours, marking the beginning of the GNR's long and important role in the East Coast route between England and Scotland.

The 'Towns' line

There then remained just two pieces of the GNR's jig-saw to put in place – the 'Towns' line between Peterborough and Retford and King's Cross station in London. Work on the former had been postponed, not only because of financial constraints but also, as stated above,

because of changes of plan. A number of Deviations Bills had both succeeded and foundered in Parliament, and as late as the autumn of 1849 suggestions for route alterations were being made by Joseph Cubitt (who was William Cubitt's son and had been appointed first as engineer for the lines between London, Peterborough and Lincoln in July 1846 and then for all works from September 1847). The GNR Directors sensibly stuck with what Parliamentary authority they already had and in September 1849 they awarded the first 'Towns' line contract that included the boring of Stoke tunnel at the summit of the GNR main line just south of Grantham. To complete the rest of the route seven further contracts were divided between five different firms, the contracts being allocated in a seemingly random order over the next eighteen months.

The 'Towns' line included the crossing of two existing railways on the level: over the MS&LR at Retford and over the MR at Newark. At the latter and shortly before

The western face of the stone and brick viaduct over the River Trent north of Newark-on-Trent. A few hundred yards behind the photographer were the cast and wrought-iron twin bridges taking the railway over the Trent Dyke. (Author's collection)

King's Cross station looking north-east from Euston Road. The photograph shows the façade as it appeared at the start of the 1870s just after Old St Pancras Road that had run immediately in front of the station had been re-routed, following the construction of St Pancras station out of sight to the left. (Author's collection)

the 'Towns' line was due to open the MR had twice removed GNR tracks from this 'flat crossing' before a truce was declared between the two companies and rails were allowed to remain in place. Despite various other problems, goods trains were able to use the 'Towns' line from 15 July 1852, and on 1 August new passenger stations opened at Tallington, Essendine, Little Bytham, Corby, Great Ponton, Grantham, Hougham, Claypole, Newark, Carlton-on-Trent, Tuxford and Retford.

King's Cross station

It was perhaps fitting that of all the works authorised by the original GNR Act of 1846 the last to be completed was the London terminus at King's Cross. When it came into use on 14 October 1852, the station was the most impressive public space in the capital and remained so until the enlarged structure of the Great

Exhibition of 1851 was reopened as the Crystal Palace at Sydenham, and the cast-iron arches of the Great Western Railway's Paddington station were unveiled in 1854.

William Cubitt had supervised the erection of the original 1851 Crystal Palace, and along with his nephew, Lewis Cubitt, had also been responsible for erecting the propylaeum at Euston (the 'Euston Arch') for the London & Birmingham Railway at the end of the 1830s. That arch was an expensive piece of theatre separated from a nondescript station behind, whereas at King's Cross, Lewis Cubitt in his role as architect had simply and economically fused together train sheds and façade to create one coherent structure. After six years and five months from the securing of its original Act, the GNR main line between London King's Cross and Yorkshire was finally complete.

THE FIRST TWENTY YEARS

The GNR was fortunate that by the end of the 1840s the pioneering days of railways had passed. Fully enclosed carriages for all classes of passenger were required by law, and reliable steam locomotives could be acquired from a number of well-respected engineering companies already supplying other main line railways.

That reliable designs of steam engines were available was fortunate as two company locomotive engineers had come and gone before the main line out of King's Cross was opened. In November 1846, Benjamin Cubitt (brother of William) had become the first Locomotive Engineer but he died in January 1848. The following month Edward Bury, founder of Bury, Curtis & Kennedy of Liverpool, was appointed, but although he was responsible for the first orders of locomotives and carriages, he resigned in February 1850.

His replacement was Archibald Sturrock who had been Works Manager since 1843 at the Swindon Works of the Great Western Railway (GWR). He inherited locomotives supplied by Bury, Curtis & Kennedy, and Sharp Brothers and William Fairbairn (both based in Manchester), and then went on to patronise R. & W. Hawthorn of Newcastle-upon-Tyne, E.B. Wilson of Leeds, Kitson & Hewitson of Hunslet, Leeds, Robert Stephenson & Co of Newcastle-upon-Tyne, The Yorkshire Engine Co. of Sheffield and John Fowler & Co. of Leeds.

For main line passenger services, locomotives with the 2-2-2 wheel arrangement became the GNR's standard type and soon earned the company a reputation for reliable, safe and speedy travel. In the 1850s Sturrock did flirt with ten 4-2-0 'Crampton' engines and

an experimental 4-2-2 (No. 215) but the Cramptons were all quickly rebuilt and No. 215 of 1853 remained a one-off. For the rest of the decade, he concentrated on

Part of a mid-1870s photograph showing the goods yard on the east (up) side and just north of Hatfield passenger station very little altered since it was brought into use in 1850. The semaphore signal with its arm pivoted in a slot at the top of the post appears to be a main line signal positioned on the 'wrong' side of the line, probably for sighting purposes. (T.W. Latchmore, Hitchin/ Author's collection)

The sixth 2-2-2 locomotive in a batch of twenty supplied to the GNR by Sharp Brothers & Co., Manchester in 1848. The class, nicknamed 'Little Sharps', eventually comprised fifty engines by 1850. This photograph (said to have been taken at Grantham in 1854) shows the engine in its original condition. (A. Jerome Ltd)

The GNR's first locomotive, built by Sharp Brothers and delivered to the railway company on 3 August 1847. This 1860s photograph shows it after it had been converted at the GNR's Boston Works to a tank engine, in which form it continued to work until April 1870, when it was withdrawn from service. (Locomotive Publishing Co./Author's collection)

No. 208, delivered to the GNR in October 1852, was one of a dozen 2-2-2 locomotives supplied by Hawthorn's, the class commonly referred to as 'Large Hawthorns' to distinguish them from the slightly smaller 2-2-2s built by that firm. By 1857 the new engines were hauling some of the fastest expresses on the main line, averaging 50.5mph between King's Cross and Hitchin, with maxima approaching 70mph.
(The Engineer 1925/Author's collection)

rebuilding earlier locomotives, and after 1855 no new engines were acquired until 1860, when twelve 2-2-2s were built to his design. These were arguably his finest passenger engines, with seven foot (2.13m) driving wheels and large boilers pressed to 150psi. Six years later he designed and had built a number of handsome 2-4-0s but these were all subsequently rebuilt as 2-2-2s by his successor, Patrick Stirling.

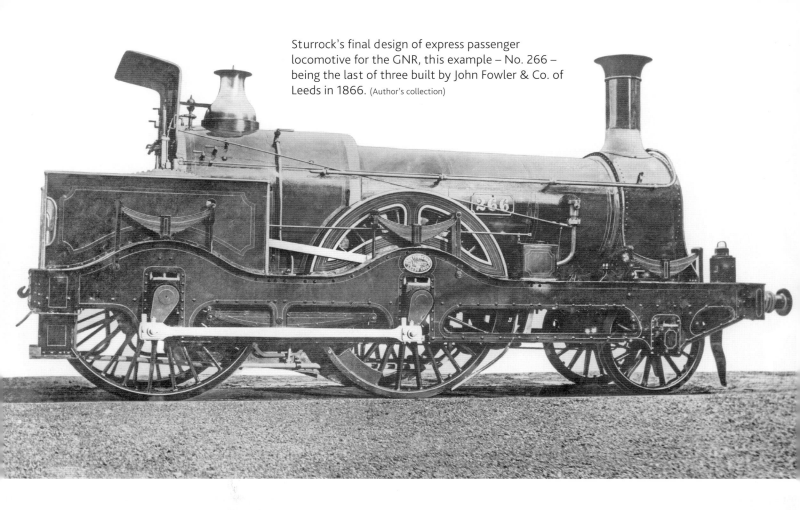

Sturrock's final design of express passenger locomotive for the GNR, this example – No. 266 – being the last of three built by John Fowler & Co. of Leeds in 1866. (Author's collection)

2-2-2 No. 267 was the first of three locomotives originally built to Sturrock's 2-4-0 design by the Yorkshire Engine Co., Sheffield at the very end of 1866. Patrick Stirling had it rebuilt in 1873 as a 2-2-2 and the engine ran in the form shown in this photograph until May 1902. (F. Moore's Photographs 9950)

For goods and mineral traffic, numerous 0-6-0s were acquired in the 1850s, and as traffic grew in the following decade Sturrock tried to increase their haulage capacity by pairing them with 'steam tenders', the wheels of which were coupled and driven by an auxiliary set of cylinders. By the end of 1865 a fleet of fifty had been created, but although more than capable, the engines were heavy on fuel and lubricating oil, needed more maintenance than conventional locomotives, and were unpopular with engine crews. After Sturrock's retirement in 1866, the tenders were stripped of their auxiliary cylinders and coupling rods, and all engines that had modified fireboxes were rebuilt.

All these rebuilds were undertaken at Doncaster Works, another of Sturrock's achievements. Plans for engine sheds and workshops there had been drawn up back in May 1848 at the same time as Boston was being developed as the main centre for locomotive repairs. This Lincolnshire location was always considered a temporary headquarters and between then and the summer of 1851, various other locations for permanent locomotive and carriage works were considered and rejected before Doncaster was confirmed as the final choice. It is known that Bury had favoured Doncaster but Sturrock thought Peterborough a more logical location, being more central to the network as it was developing. In fact it was Sturrock who was responsible for the establishment of New England, just north of Peterborough station. New England soon evolved into the company's principal location on the main line for the stabling, running, repair and maintenance of the growing fleet of goods locomotives, and around it grew a considerable township.

What was christened 'The Plant' at Doncaster became the centre for heavy repairs, the rebuilding of locomotives and the construction of carriages. By 1860 such was the reputation of coaching stock

The well known and probably only surviving photograph of the first of Sturrock's 0-6-0s attached to a 'steam tender'. Built by Kitson & Co., Hunslet, Leeds in 1864, it was rebuilt three times and not withdrawn until November 1899, more than repaying its initial cost of £3,350. (Locomotive Publishing Co./Author's collection)

Sturrock 0-6-0 No. 415, one of the Hawthorn batch of 1865 engines that were originally supplied with 'steam tenders', was still hauling mineral trains on the main line in 1900. It was photographed here emerging from the south end of Hadley Wood North Tunnel after being rebuilt with a Stirling 'straight back' boiler. (R. Brookman/Author's collection)

No. 465 was another of Sturrock's 0-6-0s intended to have a 'steam tender', but was delivered without the appropriate equipment being fitted. In this photograph, taken shortly after the engine was completed in the spring of 1866, the elaborate lining applied to the Brunswick Green of both the engine and tender is clearly visible. This, combined with a large polished brass dome and other burnished fittings, must have made for quite a colourful locomotive. (Locomotive Publishing Co./Author's collection)

built at Doncaster that in that year the works began building vehicles for use on the through London–Edinburgh services run by the GNR, North Eastern Railway (NER) (created by the amalgamation of the York & North Midland Railway, the York, Newcastle & Berwick Railway, and Leeds & Northern Railway in 1854) and the North British Railway (NBR). The GNR had proposed the use of dedicated carriages for Anglo–Scottish services and its partners had readily agreed to share the costs of having the vehicles built at Doncaster. The result was a fleet of four-wheeled carriages very similar in design and finish – varnished teak – to existing GNR vehicles but bearing the title 'East Coast Joint Stock' (ECJS) and that organisation's emblem.

The arrival side of King's Cross terminus photographed shortly after the original laminated timber roof arches had been replaced with wrought-iron in 1869–70. To the right are rows of some of the GNR's earliest four-wheeled carriage designs. (Official photograph BR16158/Author's collection)

The most famous cross-border train was 'The Flying Scotsman', the GNR running this service between King's Cross and York. It had originated in 1859 when the first 10am left Edinburgh for King's Cross, and then from June 1862 when a 10am express started to operate in the opposite direction, the two services became known collectively as the 'Special Scotch Expresses' or 'The Flying Scotchmen'. The latter title was never official but was widely recognised as applying to these two prestige expresses, timetabled in 1862 to take ten and a half hours going north and eleven and a half hours travelling south.

Relationships with other companies

The ECJS was a successful joint venture and continued to be so right up until the end of the GNR's independent existence in 1923, but it contrasted with more difficult relationships with other companies.

Given the MR's opposition to the GNR during the 'Railway Mania', it was almost inevitable that there would continue to be friction between these two organisations. From July 1850, the MR had started to share its Nottingham station with the Ambergate, Nottingham & Boston & Eastern Junction Railway (usually referred to just as the 'Ambergate'). This company had been unable to achieve its aim of linking Lancashire with the Lincolnshire coast and had to be content with a line from a junction with the MR at Netherfield just east of Nottingham to a modest terminus in Grantham. Under an agreement with the GNR the 'Ambergate' had the right to use the former's station at

Grantham when that opened, and when this took place in August 1852, along with the GNR's new 'Towns' line it triggered one of those oft-related amusing events in railway history. When an 'Ambergate' train with through carriages from King's Cross pulled into the MR's station at Nottingham behind a GNR locomotive, once detached from its train that engine was manoeuvred by MR engines into a redundant shed and the lines lifted to prevent its escape. Court proceedings followed and the GNR even approached the MR with a suggestion the two companies should amalgamate to avoid further costly conflicts. Simultaneously, an amalgamation was also proposed between the MR and the LNWR but Parliament viewed both these plans as rate-fixing exercises and was unwilling to sanction them or any further amalgamations that it felt would create competition-stifling monopolies.

The consequence of the Nottingham incident and Parliament's stance, led to a thaw in MR and GNR relations. The MR agreed to allow GNR traffic via the 'Ambergate' into Nottingham under an existing agreement in return for the GNR not opposing its Bill for a line between Leicester (Wigston) and Hitchin. This line had originally been promoted under Hudson's chairmanship with the intention that it should not join but cross the GNR at Hitchin to make a connection with a planned extension to the ECR. In 1853 the Royal Assent was secured for the new MR line that would make a connection with the GNR at Hitchin. The following year, the GNR was empowered by Act of Parliament to work the 'Ambergate' and purchase its engines and rolling stock, and in 1857 it opened its own terminus on London Road in Nottingham.

When the MR's Hitchin line opened in that same year, the company soon diverted most of its London traffic away from its old connections with the LNWR and onto the GNR main line. This included

The impressive 'roundhouse' engine shed built by the GNR for the use of the MR at King's Cross. It was brought into use in February 1859 almost exactly a year after MR trains had started to use the GNR main line between Hitchin and London. The MR vacated the premises in 1868 when its own line into St Pancras station was fully operational, after which the building was used by the GNR (as it appears in this Edwardian photograph). It was demolished in 1931.
(Locomotive Publishing Co. 1499/Author's collection)

Dunstable Church
Street station as it
appeared in the last
years before the
First World War. The
GNR had started to
run passenger trains
between Hatfield
and the town via
Luton in September
1860. The signalbox
seen here was
brought into use
in 1890. (Commercial
postcard/Author's collection)

an increasing tonnage of coal emanating from the Nottinghamshire & Derbyshire coalfield. As a consequence, the route between Hitchin and King's Cross became heavily congested and although the GNR eased its signalling regulations and planned to lay additional goods lines, the MR decided it would be better to build its own line into the capital. The Bill for this Bedford to St Pancras line was put to the Parliamentary session of 1863. It was a sensible and almost inevitable response to a growing problem but the GNR still felt obliged to oppose the plans. One reason was that it was running a branch line from its main line just north of Hatfield station at Welwyn Junction to Harpenden and Luton and had an agreement to run another to St Albans (opened 1865), all these towns to be served by the new MR

main line. Ironically, seventeen years after Hudson and his MR had opposed the London & York project, the GNR became an opponent of the MR's London line, and as Hudson had failed in his aim, so too did the GNR. The MR's 'London Extension' Act received the Royal Assent in June 1863.

To compensate for the loss of revenue from MR traffic along its main line, and irritated by the rates the company was charging for Nottingham and Derbyshire coal transferred to the 'Ambergate' at Nottingham, the GNR proposed to build its own line into the coalfield. The threat of this persuaded the MR to give the GNR better rates but the former also insisted that this agreement must cover rates for carrying coal from all the other coalfields served by the two companies. The GNR agreed and its plans were dropped

but the seeds were sown for future trouble (examined in the next chapter).

Shortly after this, the GNR and the MR were drawn into negotiations with another independent company. In 1866 the Midland & Eastern Railway (M&ER) was formed by the amalgamation of two smaller companies, enabling it to complete a route between the GNR at Bourn (at the end of its branch from the main line at Essendine), through Spalding and Sutton Bridge to Lynn. Sections of this route were already being operated on behalf of their owners by the GNR. So when another line worked by the MR reached Sutton Bridge in 1866 from a junction with its system at Peterborough through Murrow and Wisbech, the GNR and MR found themselves in an uneasy handshake. What the M&ER Amalgamation Bill had also sought was powers to build a line between Bourn and the MR at Saxby but the GNR had successfully opposed this by offering as an alternative to share the running of a service over existing lines from Bourn via Essendine to Stamford, where a new connection could be made with the MR. (The Stamford & Essendine Railway worked by the GNR had opened in November 1856.) After further negotiations, all the companies concerned agreed that the working of the line between Bourn and Lynn should be shared between the GNR and the MR and a joint committee was set up to facilitate this. This arrangement eventually led to the formation of the Midland & Great Northern Joint Railway in 1893 that is dealt with in a later chapter.

As mentioned previously, the GNR had taken advantage of good relations with the L&YR to reach Wakefield and Leeds in 1849. At the latter the GNR briefly shared the then uncompleted 'Central' station with that company and two others before withdrawing to its own temporary station in May 1850. Four years later when the Leeds, Bradford & Halifax Junction Railway opened in August 1854, a line the GNR had agreed to work, the L&YR not only allowed the GNR back into Leeds Central but also granted it running powers into its station in Halifax. Three years later another company that the GNR had agreed to work, namely the Bradford, Wakefield & Leeds Railway (BW&LR), opened its line between a junction with the L&YR at Wakefield and Holbeck Junction just outside Leeds. The GNR was then able to divert its trains from the MR Methley–Leeds line and onto the L&YR line between Pontefract and Wakefield. The BW&LR built its own station in Wakefield, calling it Westgate. Although the new route freed the GNR from its reliance on the MR, it was more circuitous, and what ultimately improved the GNR's access between Doncaster, Wakefield and Leeds, placing both the latter towns on a new and more direct main line, was co-operation with the Manchester Sheffield & Lincolnshire Railway (MS&LR).

By the early 1850s the GNR and MS&LR made very useful physical connections at Grimsby, Retford, Lincoln and Gainsborough, but due to its involvement in the so-called LNWR's 'Euston Square Confederacy', the MS&LR had been obliged to adopt obstructionist policies with regard to the handling of GNR traffic. But in 1856 during one of the periodic inter-company battles over traffic rates, the 'Confederacy' began to unravel. Its architect – the LNWR's General Manager, Mark Huish – then made an overture in May 1857 to Seymour Clarke, the GNR's General Manager, and suggested new arrangements between their companies with apparently no reference to the MS&LR. The outcome was not what Huish intended but a rift between the LNWR and the MS&LR and a new partnership between the latter company and the GNR. Compared to Huish's clandestine confederacy, the GNR and MS&LR decided on a very public declaration of their new relationship and immediately tabled a Bill to Parliament for a new 'Fifty Year Agreement'. A new service was inaugurated between King's Cross and Manchester (London Road) via Retford in direct and open competition to the

In 1854, Sturrock designed a 2-4-0 tender locomotive especially for working trains over the Leeds, Bradford & Halifax Junction Railway. Six engines of this design were built by Hawthorn's and put to work in 1855. This photograph of No. 224 at Leeds in the 1880s shows the engine rebuilt with a Stirling boiler and cab. (Author's collection)

existing trains the LNWR ran between London Euston and Manchester (London Road). For a few months the Manchester station became a battle ground, the LNWR harassing both MS&LR staff and passengers before a truce was declared and the GNR and MS&LR 'Traffic Arrangements Act' passed into law at the end of July 1858. The Manchester expresses eventually became some of the fastest trains on the GNR.

This new agreement did not, however, prevent periodic realignments of alliances. Barely two years after it came into force the GNR and LNWR suggested a joint takeover of the MS&LR. Negotiations were entered into at the end of 1860 but agreement could not be reached. Soon afterwards the MS&LR announced it was in talks with the South Yorkshire Railway (SYR) over a merger that immediately antagonised the GNR. This was because

since it opened in November 1849, the SYR had been channelling coal onto the GNR at Doncaster for transportation to London. For some years after this, the GNR had a monopoly of supplying coal to the capital by rail, and in order to protect this business, the company had arranged an amalgamation with the SYR in 1852. An Act for this was secured in June that year but Denison, the GNR's chairman, began to realise that one particular clause in the Act would allow the MR to syphon off traffic from the SYR, in effect undermining the reasons the GNR wanted an amalgamation in the first place. Consequently, he persuaded his Board not to proceed, with the result that for a time the slighted SYR stopped sending coal onto the GNR. A settlement was eventually reached but the MS&LR's move to take over the SYR at the beginning of 1861 obviously challenged the uneasy relationship between the GNR and the SYR.

The GNR's relationship with the MS&LR did, nevertheless, soon gave the former a better foothold in the West Riding of Yorkshire and in Lancashire, and access to not only the port of Grimsby but also Liverpool. In 1866, the two companies became the joint owners of the recently completed West Riding & Grimsby Railway. This new route between Doncaster and Wakefield Westgate enabled the GNR to shave twenty minutes from the old King's Cross–Leeds schedule via the L&YR lines, the fastest new service being just 4hr 35min. In anticipation of the elevated status of Wakefield on this new main line, Westgate station was rebuilt, reopening at the beginning of May 1867. In the same decade, the GNR joined forces with the MS&LR in creating the Cheshire Lines Committee (CLC). The full story of this concern cannot be told in this narrative, but sufficient to record that by the end of the period covered by this chapter new lines had connected Northwich, Stockport, Warrington, and Liverpool (Brunswick), with the network still expanding.

The last company the GNR grappled with in the 1860s was the Great Eastern Railway (GER). That company had been formed in August 1862 by the amalgamation of the ECR with a number of smaller concerns. The new GER was in no better financial shape than the ECR but it did try to project a more robust image, and in its first year it promoted a line from March to Spalding from where it sought running powers over the GNR to Doncaster in order to access the SYR and the coalfield it served. The scheme failed and Parliament found in favour of an alternative GNR plan to link March and Spalding but it did oblige the company to grant the GER running powers.

The concession, however, was insignificant compared with the GER's original intention of achieving independent access to Doncaster, and as a result, in 1864 it threw its wholehearted support behind the Great Eastern Northern Junction Railway (GENJR) project for a line purely for the transportation of coal from South Yorkshire to London. The new route was to stretch from the GER's main line just north of Cambridge, passing close to Peterborough, Sleaford, Lincoln and Gainsborough to a junction with the recently authorised West Riding & Grimsby Railway just north of Doncaster.

Fortunately for the GNR, in the same Parliamentary session it had deposited plans to complete the connection between its main line and the 'Loop' (detailed in the first chapter) and what this Gainsborough–Doncaster connection would then create was a route so similar to that proposed by the GENJR that it would completely negate that organisation's project. Parliament agreed and threw out the GENJR plans, but as a concession, the GNR had to offer the GER running rights for coal traffic along the completed 'Loop' between Doncaster and March. After another vain attempt to revive the GENJR project the following year, the GNR felt it wise to offer the GER something better than just running powers, and that is when the first proposal was made for joint ownership of the existing 'Loop' line and the new extension between March and Spalding. The eventual outcome of these deliberations is examined in the next chapter.

Probably the most unsatisfactory arrangement with the GER was over the link between Hitchin and Cambridge. Access to Cambridge from the GNR main line had been a goal for the company since it took over the powers of the Royston & Hitchin Railway in 1846. In the Parliamentary Session of 1848 that railway had also secured authority to extend its line to Shepreth, there to join the ECR's planned branch from Cambridge. Worked by the GNR, the line between Hitchin and Royston opened at the end of October 1850, with the extension to Shepreth completed in the summer of the following year. It was then agreed that once the ECR had completed

the Cambridge link, it would take over the whole route from Hitchin for fourteen years and grant the GNR access to its station at Cambridge. The through route was opened in April 1852, but in 1864, two years before the agreement was due for re-negotiation, the GNR threatened to promote its own line from Shepreth to Cambridge. This forced the new GER – who had inherited the deal – to agree to upgrade the section north of Shepreth to double-track and renew its rival's running powers to Cambridge. All this bartering came at a time when the GNR and GER were in conflict over the proposed GENJR scheme, which was soon followed by negotiations about the joint ownership of the GNR's 'Loop' line as already mentioned. Quite why such an arrangement was not proposed for the Hitchin to Cambridge (Shepreth Branch Junction) route is not clear, and considering the outcome, somewhat baffling. At the beginning of April 1866, the line between Hitchin and Shepreth was handed back to the GNR, with the section between Shepreth and Cambridge,

(yet to be doubled), remaining GER property. This divided ownership of the through route between Hitchin and Cambridge lasted until the two companies became part of the London & North Eastern Railway in 1923.

To conclude this chapter, the focus turns to London. Here the GNR made some very useful connections with other companies in its first twenty years. In March 1858 the Welwyn & Hertford Railway opened giving the GNR access to the London docks via the ECR. In 1862 a junction with the North London Railway (NLR) was brought into use at Maiden Lane, giving the GNR access to Royal Mint Street Depot in the City. In January 1863 the Metropolitan Railway (MetR) opened between Bishop's Road (Paddington) and Farringdon Street – the world's first underground railway. It was initially worked by the GWR, but after that company withdrew at short notice, Sturrock quickly modified some existing GNR locomotives to 'consume their own smoke', and put them to work at the beginning of August 1863.

In the autumn of 1863, twelve GNR engines were hired to the MetR as that company had yet to take delivery of its own locomotives. Eight of the engines were 0-6-0s, one of which – No. 138 – suffered a boiler explosion on 9 May 1864 whilst waiting to take a train out of Bishop's Road station, London. This photograph appears to show that locomotive. It is of the right class and has the shortened chimney that the GNR locomotives were fitted with during their stay on the MetR. It is also standing on a traverser in front of what is almost certainly the unique 'crescent' engine shed brought into use in 1851 at King's Cross 'Top Shed'. (Locomotive Publishing Co./Author's collection)

Two months later two connections were brought into use between the MetR and the GNR either side of King's Cross station, single tracks running through two steeply inclined tunnels. The western connection became known as the Hotel Curve as it tunnelled beneath the Great Northern Hotel. To work the trains via these connections, special 0-4-2 well tanks designed by Sturrock were built in 1865. The following year the GNR was able to work goods trains south of the Thames via a junction between the MetR and the London, Chatham & Dover Railway at Farringdon Street. With this increase in traffic, the MetR quickly decided to lay an additional pair of lines alongside its original double-track section through its King's Cross station (immediately south-east of the GNR terminus), and through Farringdon Street station to Moorgate, the latter having been reached at the end of 1865. This new section of four tracks became known as 'The Widened Lines' and was first used by GNR goods trains from the end of January 1868 and by passenger trains the following month.

THE TRANSITION YEARS OF THE 1870s

A new era in the history of the GNR was heralded by the departure of the three characters who had most influenced the development of the company since the securing of the Act of 1846. The most notable was the Chairman, Edmund Denison, who had become involved in the London and York railway proposals back in 1844, fought numerous battles with rivals and had finally been forced to resign due to poor health in December 1864. Working closely with him was Seymour Clarke, General Manager from 1850 to 1870. Along with

The GNR main line through Hatfield station as it appeared after the repositioning of the down platform (on the right) in 1864. The canopy might have been erected at the same time but certainly no later than about 1875, when this photograph was taken. The earlier preference for building canopies that covered both the platform and its adjacent track can be seen in the background. (T.W. Latchmore, Hitchin/Author's collection)

Archibald Sturrock, holding the post of Locomotive Engineer from 1850 to 1866, these two men had created the GNR's reputation for its customer service and the speed of its trains. It could be said that these three characters had nurtured the GNR through its 1850s childhood and into its adolescence in the 1860s, leaving others to take the company into its early adulthood of the 1870s.

Safety

By the end of the 1860s all GNR stations were protected by semaphore signals, but the interlocking of signals with the operation of points was not to be found everywhere on the network. Neither was block working. Interlocking and block working were only installed where thought necessary due to local conditions. At the beginning of the 1870s, however, the Board of Trade through the Railway Inspectorate was pressuring companies to adopt both, consistently, over all lines. The threat of legislation to enforce this persuaded the GNR – and other companies – to change their approach to signalling.

Balby Bridge just south of Doncaster station with its four post signal gantry. The structure must have been erected before the middle of the 1870s because the tops of all four posts show they originally had semaphore arms pivoted in slots. The arms were subsequently replaced with 'somersault' semaphores but the spectacle glasses and lamps remained where first fitted at the base of the slots. All the arms below the walkway were later additions (as was the distant signal beneath the arm in the 'off' position on the right post). (Official photograph/Author's collection)

From just sixty-four route miles (103km) controlled by the block system in 1869, by 1876 the GNR had almost 350 route miles (563.3km) so protected, and by the end of this period, the GNR had erected hundreds of new signalboxes, all with interlocking lever frames. The majority of these structures survived in use for over 100 years. With decorative barge boards on their gable ends, they were the first characteristically GNR structures, displaying what would be later termed a 'corporate identity'. The architectural features that elevated these new signalboxes from the simple huts and cabins that had preceded them only a few years earlier, were overt indicators that the GNR was taking safety more seriously and was proud to display this. Consequently, when an accident at Abbotts Ripton happened on the night of 21 January 1876, GNR management must have felt dismay after such a short period in which so much had been invested in moving from the *ad hoc* signalling arrangements of the 1860s to what they believed was a new comprehensive and safe system of traffic management.

The signalbox brought into use at Rossington station in March 1876. At least six other signalboxes on the main line between Grantham and Doncaster were built to this same design in this period, all fitted with interlocking lever frames and equipped with the electrical equipment for working the absolute block system.
(Commercial postcard./Author's collection)

This signalbox at South Elmsall on the West Riding & Grimsby Railway jointly owned by the GNR and MS&LR was one of many brick and timber signalboxes brought into use in the 1870s all over the GNR network. (Author's collection)

It is well known that the cause of the accident was the failure of the levers in the signalboxes in the area to move the semaphore arms from the 'all clear' position to 'danger' because they had become frozen in their signal post slots by compacted snow. This misled the drivers of an up coal train and two expresses into believing the line was clear. Having passed Holme signalbox where it should have stopped, a coal train was being shunted into a lay-by siding at Abbotts Ripton when it was struck, first by an up express and then a north-bound express, all running under false clear signals. Fourteen passengers were killed and over fifty injured.

In the Board of Trade report following the accident, one of the recommendations was that signals protecting the entry to block sections should normally indicate 'danger' (or 'blocked') and not 'all clear'. But even this change did not prevent another accident on the GNR two days

A photograph taken shortly after a memorial was erected at Abbotts Ripton following the accident there in January 1876. Other signalboxes known to have had the same design of windows and decorative barge boards were erected on the main line at Arlesey, Biggleswade, Sandy, Tempsford, Huntingdon and Holme between 1874 and 1876. All but Abbotts Ripton, Biggleswade North, Sandy North, and Huntingdon North remained in use for a hundred years. (Ernest Whitney, Huntingdon/Author's collection)

before Christmas 1876. A goods train was being shunted across the main line at Arlesey Sidings where there was also a small station (opened in 1860 and then rebuilt to become Three Counties station in 1886). The manoeuvre had resulted in some of the wagons becoming derailed on the main line. The home and distant signals were set to danger but because the shunting was taking place beyond (in advance of) the home signal, the line between Arlesey Sidings and Cadwell to the south was clear according to the regulations. A Manchester express entered the section and all would have been well if the driver had responded to Arlesey's distant signal at danger. Unfortunately, he did not and the train also ran on past the home signal at danger, its progress only halted by hitting the derailed wagons.

Both driver and firemen were killed, as were three passengers in the train, thirty being injured.

After the accidents the GNR changed its design of semaphore, adopting one that eliminated the possibility of the arm sticking in the clear position. This 'somersault' signal very soon became a characteristic feature all over the network. Two other vital, but not so visible, changes were also made to block working procedures and adopted by other companies as well. The first was that lines between signalboxes were assumed to be 'blocked' whether or not there was a train travelling between them, and the second was the requirement that a specified distance beyond the home signal had to be unobstructed before a train could be allowed into the section. This distance

The main line near Essendine as originally laid out in 1851–2 with just two tracks. This late Victorian photograph was taken to illustrate the use of slag ballast but the distant signal is worthy of note. On the up line in this area, with its gradient falling towards Peterborough, the positioning of distant signals was very important. When the re-signalling of the 1870s had been completed, most were over 1,000 yards (914.4m) from the signalboxes that worked them. (Author's collection)

As the GNR ran fast passenger trains it believed drivers should be given the earliest indication of the state of the line in front of them. Consequently, tall signal posts and brackets were erected in many locations along the main line, such as this one just to the north of Hornsey station fitted with somersault semaphores. (12 June 1900 Locomotive Publishing Co./ Author's collection)

beyond the home signal became known variously as the 'clearing point', 'fouling point' or 'overlap'.

The 1876 accidents had also occurred at a time when the question of how best to stop a train in an emergency was being discussed. The decade had begun with passenger trains run with several brake vans, a driver sounding his whistle if he wanted the guards to apply their brakes to slow or stop the train. There were brakes on engine tenders but not on the locomotive itself, and the principle that all the carriages of a train should have brakes – referred to as 'continuous brakes' – had not been established at this time. However, growing public concern about railway accidents had led to the setting up of a Royal Commission in 1874, and in the following year trials were organised just south-west of Newark on the MR where a number of different braking systems were fitted onto ten different trains belonging to seven different railway companies. These were run up and down at various speeds, the distances covered and the times taken to stop being

carefully measured. Amongst the British designs the equipment of two American inventors were on show: the GNR train fitted with a brake devised by J.Y. Smith and one of the MR trains fitted with another designed by George Westinghouse. The principal difference between the two systems was that although both were 'continuous', Westinghouse's automatically applied the brakes on all the train even if it became divided or the equipment failed. At the time, although superior in this respect over Smith's equipment, Westinghouse was still making modifications to his design and its apparent complexity convinced Stirling that it would need constant attention if it was to work reliably in everyday service. Consequently, Westinghouse's overtures to GNR management were unsuccessful.

The accident at Abbotts Ripton took place only six months after the Newark Trials and very quickly Smith's equipment was fitted to a number of GNR trains to test it under normal, main line running conditions. At the end of the year, Westinghouse made another appeal to the company to trial his

Beautifully decorated but with no brakes! 0-4-2 No. 70 was originally built as a 2-2-2 by Hawthorn & Co. in 1850 and rebuilt in May 1870. Posed here at Hitchin a few years later it was subsequently fitted with Smith's simple vacuum brake, and then automatic brakes, and was not withdrawn until January 1901. (Author's collection)

A North London Railway suburban train passing Finsbury Park No. 7 signalbox on the Highgate branch and about to cross over the GNR main line before pulling into the station at Finsbury Park. The signalbox was one of a number provided when the station and layout were enlarged in the 1870s. (Author's collection)

improved automatic apparatus, but once again it met with a lukewarm response from Stirling. By the end of 1877 the trials with Smith's equipment led to a definite policy of fitting all GNR engines and trains with that form of continuous but non-automatic vacuum brake.

London suburban traffic growth

By the mid-1860s the GNR was witnessing the first stages of a new phenomenon that was later to be called 'commuting'. New housing was spreading ever northwards from London, the railways enabling people to live further from their places of work and travel daily to and from home using what became known at the time as 'workmen's trains'.

The most visible evidence of this new 'suburban' traffic was the large station

and complex of lines that developed at Finsbury Park. From modest beginnings in July 1861 as Seven Sisters Road, the station was enlarged two years after the opening in August 1867 of the Highgate, Finchley & Edgware line that branched off there. In January 1870 the station acquired its new name and very soon extensive rebuilding was necessary once again to cope with traffic from three new branches. In April 1872 the High Barnet line opened, followed in May 1873 by a branch to Muswell Hill and Alexandra Palace. Under construction at the same time was a connection just south of Finsbury Park to Canonbury on the North London Railway (NLR). This connection had initially been intended to divert commuter traffic away from King's Cross and into the NLR's terminus at Broad Street but due to the influence of the LNWR

The following advertising hoarding text is visible on the platform wall:

SAUCE · WATSONS SOAP · TIT-BITS · WRIGHTS COAL TAR SOAP · EPPS'S COCOA · OETZMANN & Co. · SUTTON'S SEEDS · COCOA

on that company this plan was thwarted, and instead the GNR agreed that the NLR could run its trains through Finsbury Park to and from Broad Street. These services began from January 1875.

As well as all this new traffic GNR tracks on the approaches to London were also having to cope with workmen's trains run by the London, Chatham & Dover Railway (LC&DR) between Barnet, Enfield and Finsbury Park and Victoria, and those of the South Eastern Railway (SER) between Enfield and Greenwich. All these passed through King's Cross station and the links there to the MetR. And added to the mix after Christmas 1873 were trains to and from the GNR's new Farringdon Street Goods Station.

The result was severe congestion between New Barnet and King's Cross. Relief lines had been laid at various places but the bottlenecks were Maiden Lane or Gas Works and Copenhagen tunnels. In

August 1877 an additional double-track Copenhagen tunnel on the west side of the original bore was completed and immediately at its north end the up (south-bound) goods line was taken over the main line tracks on skew bridges. Taking the up goods line from the east to the west side of the main lines here meant that the inconvenience of having to cross all south-bound goods trains over the main line at Belle Isle (at the south end of the original tunnel) could be ended. In March 1878 a new double-track Maiden Lane or Gas Works tunnel was brought into use and in connection with this, the 1863 platform used by suburban trains on the link with the MetR north-east of the train sheds at King's Cross was removed and replaced by a proper small station – York Road. Improvements for local passengers were also carried out on the opposite side of the main terminus where King's Cross Suburban station was taking shape.

King's Cross Suburban station in the form it had assumed by the end of the 1870s. Looking from the 'Hotel Curve' platform on the link between the GNR and Metropolitan Railway's underground lines, this 1893 photograph was taken shortly before the station was rebuilt. (J. Braithwaite–V.R. Webster, Kidderminster Railway Museum collection 020617)

Nottinghamshire, Derbyshire, Staffordshire and Leicestershire

Arguably the boldest project undertaken by the GNR since securing its original 1846 Act was expansion into the Nottinghamshire and Derbyshire coalfield. The impetus was yet another spat with the MR which began at the close of the 1860s. The details cannot be expanded upon in this book but sufficient to relate that the MR, GNR, MS&LR, GER and LNWR were all drawn into the inter-company warfare that broke out.

A Bill for the GNR's 'Derbyshire & Staffordshire Extension' project was put before Parliament in 1872. The line was to branch off from the Nottingham–Grantham line at Colwick, circle Nottingham and then run northwards up the Erewash valley to Pinxton, barely losing sight of the MR's main line in this location. At the point where the line turned up the Erewash valley, another line would continue westwards through the heart of the MR's empire at Derby to a junction with the North Staffordshire Railway (NSR) at Egginton just north of Burton-on-Trent, from where that company agreed to grant running powers into this brewing centre. So well presented and with positive support in Derby and from colliery owners, the Royal Assent was granted for both routes in July 1872.

Around this project swirled others, some provoking outright opposition from the GNR, others leading to compromises and eventual joint working arrangement.

The first two miles of the GNR's 'Derbyshire & Staffordshire Extension' line north from Colwick Yard to Mapperley Tunnel was on a continuously rising gradient, mostly of 1 in 100. This photograph shows the 3.50pm iron ore train from Colwick in July 1912 tackling that incline on its way to the blast furnaces of Stanton Ironworks. The GNR built its branch to that ironworks in 1885. (F.H. Gillford/Author's collection)

Over the next two years there were proposals and counter proposals to create new north–south routes, all failing in their original forms, and adding to the mix, the South Yorkshire Railway was formally absorbed by the MS&LR in July 1874. Eventually the GNR emerged with powers to extend southwards from the main line at Newark to Bottesford approximately half way along the Nottingham and Grantham line, there to join forces with the LNWR in the construction of a line southwards through Melton Mowbray and on to a junction with the LNWR just north of Market Harborough. From this Great Northern & London North Western Joint (GN&LNW Joint) line, the GNR secured powers to build its own line to Leicester.

The first coal trains emerged from the Erewash Valley along GNR lines in August 1875, running into a new marshalling yard at Colwick. Passenger services began modestly in February the following year, the full service between the terminus at Pinxton and Nottingham London Road terminus starting in August 1876. The extension to Derby and the junction with the NSR at Egginton were ready for traffic at the start of 1878, initially for goods

and minerals in January and then for passengers from April.

Two years later the GNR consolidated its position in the Nottinghamshire coalfield by constructing a line up the Leen Valley where new deep coalmines had opened or were in the process of being sunk. The first coal trains used this new route in the summer of 1881, and a passenger service to and from Nottingham inaugurated at the beginning of October the following year. By then what might be considered the western extremity of the GNR's 'Derbyshire & Staffordshire Extension' railway had become the company's property. This was the Stafford & Uttoxeter Railway (S&UR), a single-track line that had opened a few days before Christmas 1867. It branched off the NSR's Stoke-on-Trent and Uttoxeter line to the west of the latter town and then joined the LNWR just north of its main line station in Stafford. The GNR took over the S&UR in August 1881 and was thereby able to run its trains to Stafford; an agreement was reached with the LNWR to use its station there.

The GNR's 'Derbyshire & Staffordshire Extension' railway had been an expensive line to construct. The civil engineering was

The terminus of the GNR's Erewash Valley line at Pinxton with its small engine shed to the right and turntable behind the locomotive. When the passenger service started between Nottingham, London Road and Pinxton at the beginning of August 1876, there were nine trains each way and three on Sundays. (F.H. Gillford/ Author's collection)

The mining settlement of Eastwood was served by a station on the GNR's 'Derbyshire & Staffordshire Extension' line. Due to the Requirements of the Board of Trade current at the time, two signalboxes had to be provided at this location, the South box shown here built with a very distinctive style of barge board by the signalling contractors, McKenzie & Holland of Worcester. The North box had different barge boards and was built by the GNR's own labour but equipped by the Worcester firm! (Detail from official photograph/Author's collection)

Ilkeston station on the GNR's 'Derbyshire & Staffordshire Extension' lines as it appeared in the immediate pre-First World War years. By then it was not only dealing with passenger services between Grantham, Newark, Nottingham, Derby and Stafford, but services along the Heanor branch that started in July 1891. (WHS Kingsway Real Photo Series/Author's collection)

Although this photograph can be precisely dated to 26 March 1911 and the train identified as the 11.15am from Basford & Bulwell, the 0-4-2 No. 577 (built in 1876) and its train would have been typical sights on the GNR's 'Derbyshire & Staffordshire Extension' lines in the 1870s. (R.K. Blencowe Historic Railway Photos)

Heanor Road bridge at the east end of Ilkeston station, both the road and footbridges built for the completion of the GNR's 'Derbyshire & Staffordshire Extension' lines in 1878. (Detail from official photograph/Author's collection)

With the development of Colwick Yard, and as the settlement around it and the engine sheds began to grow, Colwick station became a busy place. A few months after a passenger service started to run along the GNR's Leen Valley line in 1882, the station was renamed Netherfield & Colwick, the ever cost-conscious company retaining the original four-sided station name boards and simply attaching a new and more modest double-sided addition. (Detail from official photograph/Author's collection)

extensive. It required numerous bridges, embankments and cuttings to take it across the grain of the land including the 500yds (457.2 metres) long and 60ft (18.3 metres) high Bennerley viaduct and it had to be fully signalled to meet the latest requirements of the Board of Trade. But despite this, the revenue generated from coal traffic along it and the parallel Leen Valley line more than compensated for the initial outlay, and of all the GNR's new lines built in the 1870s they were the most financially rewarding.

The extension into Leicestershire proved less remunerative. The GNR's Newark–Bottesford section that opened for goods

in April 1878 and passengers in July that year, and the line to Leicester which opened for goods in May 1882 and for passengers in October that year, probably never repaid the investment made in them. Of the two partners in the joint line, the LNWR undoubtedly benefitted the most. By granting it running powers between Doncaster, Newark and Bottesford, and into Nottingham, the GNR had enabled it to divert South Yorkshire and Erewash Valley coal that might otherwise have travelled down the GNR main line to London, into its system at Market Harborough for the journey to the capital.

Lincolnshire

Another railway the GNR felt it had to come to terms with to prevent it establishing a new north–south route for coal traffic was the GER. As related in the previous chapter, this company had backed the Great Eastern Northern Junction Railway project of 1864 and then in the storm that had given birth to the GNR's 'Derbyshire & Staffordshire Extension', had flirted with the MS&LR to reach the South Yorkshire coalfield. Serious proposals for an amalgamation between the GNR and GER came to nothing and so at the end of the 1870s, agreement was reached to create a new joint line, most of it through Lincolnshire, by utilising existing lines, upgrading others and building new ones. The GNR's lines between March and Spalding and the 'Loop' between Lincoln and Black Carr Junction, Doncaster via Gainsborough, became part of this new route; a new line was constructed between Spalding and Lincoln via Sleaford and the GER's existing lines between Huntingdon and St Ives, and Needingworth Junction (just north of the latter) and March were upgraded. The Act for all this was secured in July 1879, and the last section of the completed Great Northern & Great Eastern Joint Railway (GN&GE Joint) was opened throughout for goods in July 1882 and for passengers the following month. As part

of the scheme, 'avoiding' lines were constructed at Sleaford and Lincoln so that goods and mineral trains did not have to travel through the passenger stations there. This was particularly necessary at Lincoln as there had been complaints about road traffic being held up at the level crossings on High Street and Pelham Street ever since the GNR arrived in the city at the end of the 1840s.

On a more modest scale, the GNR also started to work two single-track independent lines in Lincolnshire in this period, which increased in importance over the years. The Wainfleet & Firsby Railway opened for goods in September 1871 and then passengers the following month, but its true worth came once the line had been extended to Skegness in July 1873. It quickly became apparent that families from the Midlands wanted to get to the seaside, and in anticipation of increasing patronage when the GNR's new route into the Nottinghamshire coalfield and Derby was opened, the company built a connection from the Nottingham & Grantham line (at Allington Junction) to the Barkston–Boston line at Barkston East Junction to enable trains to run through between Nottingham and Skegness without any reversals *en route*. The new connection was brought into use in October 1875. Two years later a few

The GNR's terminal station on Belgrave Road, Leicester. A handful of through services were operated to and from Grantham, Newark, Peterborough and Northampton, and during holiday times, excursions to the seaside. (Commercial postcard/Author's collection)

Halifax 'Old Station' as it was called, shared by the L&YR and GNR and photographed after enlargement in 1895–6. (Commercial postcard/Author's collection)

The GNR's 1880 station in Dewsbury. When the GNR reached the town in 1874 it was already served by two other stations, one provided by the London & North Western Railway in 1848 and the other by the Lancashire & Yorkshire Railway in 1867. (WHS Kingsway Real Photo Series/Author's collection)

Stirling 0-6-0 saddle tank No.903 crossing Hewenden Viaduct just south of Cullingworth on the line between Queensbury and Keighley in June 1920. The viaduct over Harden Beck, a tributary of the River Aire, was 343yds (313.6m) long and approximately 123ft (37.5m) at its highest above the valley and was one of the numerous substantial pieces of GNR civil engineering in the West Riding of Yorkshire. (J.E. Kite)

New locomotives

Patrick Stirling took over at Doncaster in October 1866, at a time when the Board had lost faith with the department and was probably relieved that Archibald Sturrock had tendered his resignation. As a result, Stirling was appointed for a trial period of only three years. He had been Locomotive Engineer for the Glasgow & South Western Railway since 1853 and, therefore, had spent almost exactly the same time in charge of locomotive design and running as Sturrock. Both men had experimented during that period but Stirling had the advantage because he came to the GNR with that behind him.

There was a period of transition when Sturrock and Stirling were together at Doncaster, but after the former's departure Stirling found himself completely in tune with the Board: they wanted a better managed and less costly locomotive department and Stirling sought simplicity in design and the use of as many interchangeable parts between locomotives as possible. One of the most visible manifestations of this economical approach was the 'straightback' boiler. Without a dome its outline was simple but, more importantly, it was cheaper to

construct than those of Sturrock's design. The only embellishment was a conical brass cover over the safety valves. As well as those engines he inherited and rebuilt, Stirling's locomotives were based on only half a dozen simple wheel arrangements: 4-2-2, 2-2-2, 2-4-0, 0-6-0, 0-4-2, and 0-4-4, the first two exclusively for passenger traffic. To better control the uniformity of design and construction of all these locomotives, Stirling had little problem persuading the Board that all locomotives should be built in-house rather than supplied by outside contractors on the basis of the lowest tender. A number of his first designs (and a few others in later years) were not built at Doncaster but once the very first all new 0-4-2 had appeared from there at the beginning of January 1868, 'The Plant' was transformed from a repair and maintenance works into one of the country's major locomotive manufacturing centres, remaining so until the last quarter of the twentieth century.

The most famous of all Doncaster products was, of course, Stirling's '8ft single'. This design became synonymous with the GNR and its reputation for running fast trains, and of all Stirling's designs it was this 4-2-2 that brought

This engine had originally been supplied by Kitson & Co., Hunslet, Leeds in May 1860, the first in a batch of four of this Sturrock design of 2-2-2 constructed by that firm. It was rebuilt by Stirling and eventually placed on the duplicate list in July 1886 as 229A. It was finally withdrawn in July 1897. (Locomotive Publishing Co./Author's collection)

This 2-2-2 No. 6 was the first in a batch of six built in 1868 to a Stirling design, eliminating what the designer perceived were the short-comings of Sturrock's 2-2-2 locomotives. Stirling's No. 6 was also significant in being only the fourth engine built at Doncaster Works. By the time this photograph was taken, the side window in its original cab had been plated over. (Locomotive Publishing Co. 16189/Author's collection)

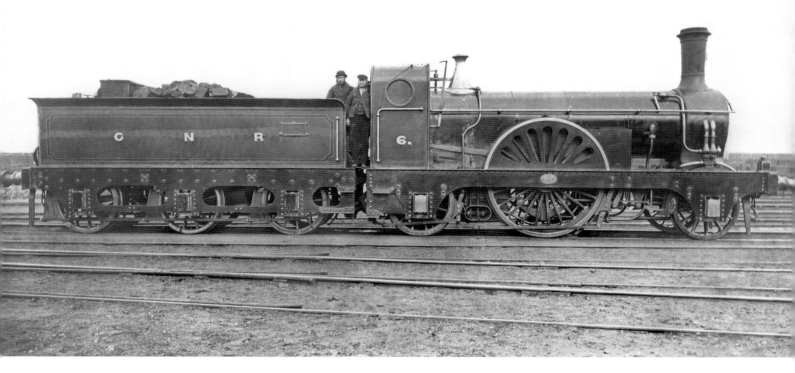

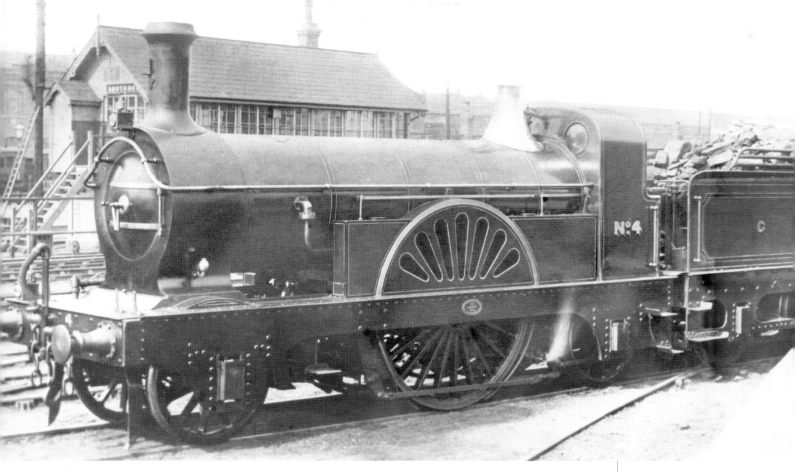

In 1867 Stirling obtained Board approval to build replacements for old engines at 'The Plant'. This accounts for the re-allocation of existing numbers to Doncaster-built locomotives. No. 4, for example, (seen here at Doncaster), was a replacement of Sharp's 2-2-2 No. 4 of 1848, withdrawn in June 1868. It was not until 1873 that the Board sanctioned the building of completely new engines that were not replacements for earlier machines. (Author's collection)

For working the easy and short Stamford & Essendine branch line, Stirling designed a small saddle tank locomotive, of which No. 501 seen here at Essendine was the first of half a dozen built between 1876 and 1878. No. 501 was photographed in July 1904 after brake gear had been added and its cab had been modified. (W.J. Reynolds/ Locomotive Club of Great Britain – Ken Nunn Collection H1294)

him and the company the most prestige and with which his name will be forever linked. The prototype, the appropriately numbered No. 1, emerged from Doncaster Works in April 1870. Approval for a locomotive with the same wheel arrangement as Sturrock's experimental one-off of 1853 coincided with the official end of Stirling's probationary period, at which time he must have felt confident he had the unequivocal support of the Board. The new engine was not an immediate success and the initial teething problems might explain the existence of a drawing from the same period of an outside cylinder 4-4-0. But the alterations made to No. 8 turned out from 'The Plant' at the end of 1870, and its twin, No. 33, put into service a few months later, quickly established the fundamental soundness of Stirling's single driving wheel design. By the end of the decade a further twenty-three '8-footers' had been built. The GNR's reputation for speed was secured and enhanced by these engines, with schedules requiring average speeds of over 50mph, easily maintained with the light trains of the period.

A well-known photograph but worth reproducing again as good quality shots of GNR expresses at speed before the end of the nineteenth century are rare. Here '8ft single' No. 60 of 1878 races the 'Special Scotch Express' southwards through Sandy on 1 August 1887, the safety valves just lifting on its replacement boiler fitted the previous year, one and a half inches (38cm) larger in diameter than its original 4ft ½in (1.223m) one! (Cameron Swan/Author's collection)

A rare photograph of Stirling '8ft single' No. 33 in its original condition without brakes. (Author's collection)

Stirling '8ft single' No. 665 photographed pulling away from the south end of Boston station. Although the locomotive was built in 1881 and the photograph taken almost ten years after that date, this image can confidently be used to illustrate a typical GNR scene of the late 1870s. (F. Moore Railway Photographs 9934/Author's collection)

CONSOLIDATION – THE 1880s AND EARLY 1890s

Passenger services

By the end of the 1870s, Patrick Stirling had created an efficient fleet of locomotives. As well as his own designs, he had rebuilt many Sturrock engines and even a number of earlier machines rebuilt by that engineer. His express engines were well able to run reliably and at speed when necessary, and those intended for secondary duties and the numerous 0-6-0 goods engines were just as dependable and all economical to maintain. The pride of the stud were of course, the '8ft singles' and in 1887 the forty-fifth member of the class was completed at Doncaster Works. Of their equal, however, was a new class of 2-2-2 locomotives, the first appearing in 1885.

Photographed at Boston station towards the end of its career at the turn of the twentieth century, Stirling '8ft single' No. 778 turned out from Doncaster Works in 1887 exhibits all the elegance and pride of the Stirling era of the 1870s and 1880s. (F. Moore Railway Photographs/Author's collection)

They looked almost exactly like Stirling's 2-2-2s of 1868 but with all the main dimensions increased by just a few inches. All these apparently small increments produced locomotives whose performance matched that of the eight-footers.

A demonstration of what these two classes of express locomotive could achieve was afforded in what became known as the 'Race to Edinburgh'. In November 1887, the GNR had finally allowed third class passengers to travel in the 'Special Scotch Express' or 'Flying Scotsman' trains. As the Anglo–Scottish services on the East Coast route took just nine hours to complete their journeys compared with the fastest West Coast trains that took ten hours, in order not to lose all its third class travellers, the partners in the latter reduced their services to a nine hour schedule as from the beginning of June 1888. It illustrates how much prestige there was attached to these trains that the East Coast companies felt compelled to respond, and the following month brought their times down to eight and a half hours. This tit-for-tat continued until an East Coast timing of seven hours thirty-two minutes was advertised for

14 August, at which point the rivals called a truce. In October after the dust had settled, they agreed to an eight-and-a-half-hour schedule for their respective 10am Anglo–Scottish services.

Although this was a memorable one-off event, the schedules of other GNR main line passenger services were also improved during the 1880s, the company being determined to retain its reputation for speed and punctuality. From July 1884, for example, the King's Cross–Manchester service run in conjunction with the MS&LR came down to just 4hr 15min. On the GNR section of the journey, the average speed was almost 54mph and could involve speeds of over 70mph down Stoke Bank, south of Grantham. In July 1888, the GNR's best time between London and Leeds came down to 3hr 52min, with the fastest journey in the opposite direction reduced from 4hr 5min to 3hr 50min.

Included in this train were Bradford and Halifax through carriages, typical features of their time. The GNR provided many such through carriages from London and other major centres to all corners of its network. Carriages were

The second of Stirling's 'improved' 2-2-2s, No. 232 was turned out from Doncaster Works in August 1885. The diaper patterns on the cab and parts of the frame were the streaks left by the rags used to polish the engine. Nos. 233, 234 & 237 of the same class took part in the 1888 'Race to Edinburgh', hauling the 10am 'Special Scotch Express' from King's Cross to Grantham in a few minutes less than two hours at average speeds of between 53.1 and 60.2mph. (F. Moore Railway Photographs 5362/Author's collection)

One of Stirling's '8ft singles' that took part in the 1888 'Race' was No. 777, seen here speeding northwards through Hitchin. It ran on six consecutive days between 6 and 11 August, taking the 10am 'Special Scotch Express' from King's Cross on to York from Grantham at midday. With a load of between 120 and 150 tons booked to complete the journey in an hour and a half, it arrived between one and three minutes early at York every day apart from the first, consistently averaging 55.1mph apart from on the last day when the average was only 54.5mph. (Author's collection)

either 'slipped' from moving trains or detached from through services as they stopped at stations. As just a few other examples of what was available in the 1880s, Lincoln could be reached from London in 2hr 45min by one of the nine services provided by slip coaches detached at Grantham, return services taking a few minutes longer. During the summer months there were through carriages between King's Cross, Scarborough and Whitby, and by the end of the decade Cromer (see below) had five services of through carriages from King's Cross, the best journey to the coast taking 4hr 15min, with a return working taking 4hr 30min.

As main line services changed in the 1880s, so too did the carriages making up the trains. In 1881, in addition to many older four-wheeled carriages, the GNR had 525 six-wheeled vehicles, eighteen bogie carriages and five Pullman cars

in service. The GNR's first carriage mounted on bogies had been turned out from Doncaster Works in 1875, one of a pair built as a response to the introduction the previous year of the first bogie Pullman cars imported from the USA for use on the MR. The GNR's Locomotive Committee suggested more should be built but Stirling was able to quell their enthusiasm on the grounds of expense and the unnecessary weight they added to a train. Despite this a few more bogies carriages were built at Doncaster in 1877, and in August 1878 the East Coast partners started running a couple of Pullman sleeping cars, *India* and *Germania*, on Anglo–Scottish services. That same year one of the MR Pullman cars was converted for use on the GNR, renamed *Prince of Wales*, and put into service between Leeds and London in November 1879 as the country's first dining car. Then in the spring of 1880

In 1882 the GNR Board was obviously convinced of the commercial merits of opening a new station barely a mile north of the existing country station at Carlton-on-Trent on the main line. Brought into use in the heart of the village of Sutton-on-Trent in November that year it was christened after a nearby farm – Crow Park – the same name conferred on the signalbox when that opened in 1875. (Commercial postcard/Author's collection)

In November 1885 a station was opened at Abbotts Ripton. The original signalbox from where the signalman had witnessed the 1876 accident continued in use there until replaced in 1892 by the signalbox in this photograph.
(Commercial postcard/ Author's collection)

Three Counties station replaced the 1860s Arlesey Sidings station at the same location. The name – taken from the nearby asylum – was officially applied in July 1886, obviously acknowledging the station's rebuilding with two long island platforms, the down slow line in the foreground having been brought into use in the same year. (Commercial postcard/Author's collection)

E.F. Howlden was one of a number of men who had long and distinguished careers with the GNR. Starting in Doncaster's carriage works in the 1850s he eventually became Carriage & Wagon Superintendent in January 1877 and did not retire until 1904. Carriages of his designs are seen here at Carcroft & Adwick-le-Street station on the West Riding & Grimsby Railway. (Commercial postcard/Author's collection)

With carriages of Howlden's design, one of Stirling's 1885 class of 2-2-2s heads towards Welwyn North Tunnel with a down train. The engine had been climbing since a mile beyond Hatfield on the 1 in 200 rising gradient but had less than one mile left before the almost continuous descent from Knebworth to Sandy. (Locomotive Publishing Co. 1651/Author's collection)

Former Pullman sleeping car *Iona* after it had been converted into Dining Car No. 2992. Apart from the gangway connection at the left end the carriage looked the same as when it started to run in April 1880. Acquired by the GNR in 1884 it continued as a sleeping carriage until December 1901 after which a kitchen was fitted so it could serve as a dining car. (Doncaster official photograph 626)

two additional Pullman sleeping cars, *Columba* and *Iona*, were run in Anglo-Scottish services.

Apart from the bogies, the other feature that made the Pullmans different from existing GNR stock was that they were not divided into compartments only accessible from the outside of the carriages. The GNR's first ordinary carriage built with an internal corridor emerged from Doncaster Works in May 1883. It was a first class, six-wheeled coach with lavatories at either end, and other vehicles with this arrangement were subsequently built for third class passengers. The development of carriages with corridors and connected together with gangways is examined in the next chapter.

The suburban problem

The increase in passenger traffic in and out of King's Cross continued to exercise GNR management in the 1880s. Despite

The wooden staging at the north end of the arrival side of King's Cross terminus in 1870 after work had just been completed on installing replacement wrought-iron roof arches. The staging was used again during 1886 and 1887 when the down side laminated timber arches were similarly replaced. (Official photograph BR16159/ Author's collection)

the duplication of Copenhagen and Maiden Lane or Gas Works tunnels at the end of the 1870s and the laying of various sections of additional track in that decade, the stretch of the main line between King's Cross and Potters Bar remained a considerable operational challenge. There was debate as to whether to continue to lay extra track or build a completely separate relief line from somewhere in the city suburbs to somewhere north of Digswell Viaduct and the tunnels at Welwyn.

Although the latter would avoid the expense of duplicating the viaduct and tunnels at Welwyn the decision was taken to widen the existing lines and an Act of Parliament was obtained for that in 1882. Over the next ten years, the appearance of the main line from north of Copenhagen tunnels to New Barnet station (renamed from just Barnet in May 1884) was transformed, with much of the infrastructure created in that period remaining intact into the 1970s.

LOCATION	WORK	BROUGHT INTO USE
Harringay station	new station (with booking hall over the tracks)	May 1885
Hadley Wood	new station (with booking hall over the tracks)	May 1885
Copenhagen Tunnel	additional double-track tunnel	June 1886
Wood Green Tunnel	additional single-track up line tunnel	March 1888 (goods), August 1888 (passengers)
Wood Green station	enlargement	Spring 1890
New Southgate station	enlargement (with booking hall over the tracks)	June 1890
Wood Green Tunnel	additional single-track down line tunnel	April 1890
Barnet Tunnel (Oakleigh Park)	additional single-track up line tunnel	October 1890 (goods)
Maiden Lane or Gas Works Tunnel	additional double-track tunnel	June 1892
Barnet Tunnel (Oakleigh Park)	additional single-track down line tunnel	June 1892

The north end of Harringay station with Stirling's 0-4-4 tank No. 939 about to depart with a suburban train. This was one of twenty-nine locomotives of this class designed in 1889 with condensing apparatus for working over the Metropolitan Railway's underground lines.
(Author's collection)

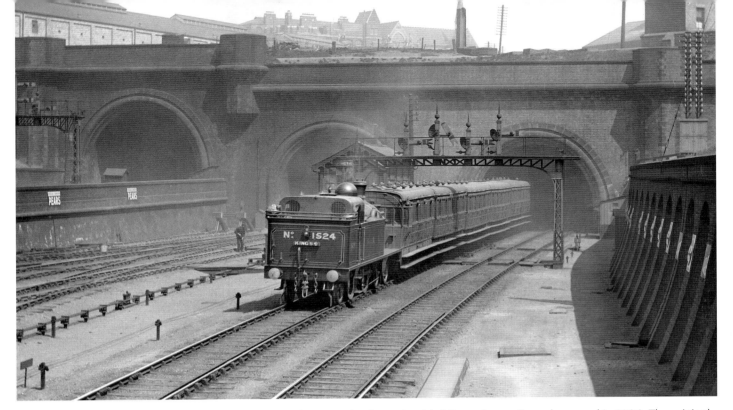

An up suburban morning service emerging from the third Copenhagen Tunnel, opened in 1886. The original 1850 bore is partly obscured by the locomotive and signalbox, whilst on the far left, at a slightly higher level, is the 1877 tunnel used exclusively for goods and mineral trains to and from King's Cross goods yard out of sight on the far left. (F. Moore Railway Photographs 2158/Author's collection)

A down express hauled by 4-4-0 No. 1376 emerging from the 1850 Barnet Tunnel and heading for Oakleigh Park station. In the background is the up slow line disappearing into the single track tunnel brought into use in 1890 and in the foreground the down slow line brought into use two years later. (Author's collection)

The provision of additional tracks north from New Barnet through Hadley Wood to Potters Bar, however, was never achieved by the GNR, this work being left to British Railways to complete in the 1950s.

Goods and minerals

During the 1880s the amount of goods carried by the GNR increased steadily despite fluctuating supply and demand. The transport of milk from country

The GNR's first station serving Ossett opened at the beginning of April 1862 and was replaced exactly two years later by a permanent station when the line was extended to Batley. It was rebuilt again in 1889 into the form shown in this photograph. The crowded goods yard shows how important the railways were to the woollen industries of the West Riding. (Lens of Sutton Association)

One of the numerous coal trains that made their way from the collieries of South Yorkshire, Nottinghamshire and Derbyshire to London, passing though Sandy station on a perfect summer evening. (Commercial postcard/ Author's collection)

The London end of the GNR's 'coal chain' at Ferme Park seen here looking south towards Hornsey station. When this photograph was taken the yard had just been enlarged between 1893 and 1900, including the provision of a number of new signalboxes erected to control the complex. (Locomotive Publishing Co. 2423-3708/Author's collection)

Stirling 0-6-0 No. 745 constructed by Dubs & Co. of Polmadie, Glasgow in 1882. It is seen with 'ballast breaks' at either end of an engineering train. These vehicles were designed and built at Doncaster especially for such trains. (Author's collection)

stations and particularly from Staffordshire to London, for example, became a major undertaking in this period. Most of the milk churns were unloaded at Finsbury Park station, where almost 50,000 were dealt with in 1884.

Responding to the growth of coal traffic, the already extensive marshalling yard at Colwick was considerably enlarged twice in the 1880s, including the provision of a new locomotive shed for the stabling of fifty engines along with associated workshops. By the end of the decade Colwick was dealing with over 1,500,000 tons of minerals annually, the majority being coal. To improve the handling of goods arriving in London from the north, a new yard at Ferme Park, Hornsey was

brought into use at the beginning of 1888. If further evidence was needed as to the amount of goods handled by the GNR in this period, by the end of the 1880s the company had on its books 18,250 open wagons, 1,250 vans, and amongst other 'specialist' vehicles, 630 cattle wagons.

Signalling and safety

The period covered by this chapter witnessed the replacement of all but a very few pieces of pre-block working signalling equipment. Hundreds of new signalboxes with fully interlocked lever frames and single needle block instruments and bells appeared all over the GNR's system, and the somersault signal replaced all pre-1876 semaphores. The London suburban work

The main line between Grantham and Doncaster was mostly double track, so to increase the capacity of that section five additional signalboxes were brought into use at various places between 1882 and 1888. Cromwell box between Muskham and Carlton-on-Trent was one of them. (Author's collection)

mentioned above entailed the erection of numerous new signalboxes, the total increased by the provision in many locations of dedicated boxes for up and down traffic. The majority of these new signalboxes were all timber structures devoid of decorative bargeboards, a significant visual break from those mainly brick-based buildings of the 1870s. Gone was the belief that signalling was a one-off investment, replaced by an understanding that layouts would have to change over time and simpler signalboxes would be not only cheaper to build but could be relocated if necessary.

In 1882, the GNR suffered from another accident that, as with those at Abbotts Ripton and Arlesey, led to changes in signalling procedures nationwide. On 10 December that year, in the morning rush hour, an engine became disabled at Dalston station on the NLR, resulting in trains being held at signals as far back as Canonbury Junction where the connection was made to Finsbury Park on the GNR. Unaware of this, when the GNR signalman at Finsbury Park No. 1 received an unfamiliar bell code from the NLR signalman at Canonbury Junction in response to his offer of a train, he misinterpreted its meaning. Rather than indicating the line was occupied, he thought it gave him permission to send the train forward after displaying a flag to indicate permissive working to the driver. Within the space of an hour, he allowed five trains into the intervening Canonbury Tunnel. Three were wrecked, the fifth only just prevented from adding to the crush by the guard of the second train running back with his lamp and detonators. The guard and four passengers in the third train lost their lives and a total of 132 were injured. The accident precipitated a review of all the bell codes in use on Britain's railways and soon led to the Railway Clearing House issuing a set of seventeen standard ones that all companies were prepared to adhere to. The GNR started to use these new codes from the beginning of October 1884.

By the end of the 1880s the GNR had almost completed the equipping of all its lines with the block system, which was just as well because, following the tragic accident near Armagh in June 1889 when over eighty passengers, many of them children, lost their lives in a runaway train, legislation was finally brought in obliging all British railway companies to run their passenger services only over lines protected by the absolute block system. The Act also stipulated that all passenger trains had to be fitted with continuous automatic brakes. The GNR had started to replace its Smith's simple vacuum brakes with new Gresham & Craven automatic equipment two years earlier. Smith's equipment had been capable of being 'upgraded' to work automatically, but after a number of trials with other systems, Stirling had advised the GNR Board that it should be replaced completely. By the close of 1892, all GNR passenger trains were equipped with Gresham & Craven gear and because the NER had adopted the Westinghouse air brake, all ECJS had both types fitted.

Commitments at the margins
In the 1880s the GNR, as in the 1870s, still felt it necessary to become involved in the working of other minor companies' lines, and two were added to the portfolio in this period. The Sutton & Willoughby Railway & Dock Co opened in October 1886 and the Nottingham Suburban Railway opened in the very last month of 1889. The former's proposed dock at Sutton-on-Sea was never built, but the line's extension to Mablethorpe, opened in July 1888, probably proved a better long term investment because, by making the seaside resort accessible from the south, a more direct and shorter journey via Sleaford could be provided for holiday-makers from the East Midlands. In the same period the GNR had also been drawn into the building of the Halifax High Level Railway from a junction at Holmfield on its existing route from Bradford into the town to a new terminus at St Paul's.

This iron, double-track bridge was brought into use across the River Witham at Grand Sluice, Boston in May 1885. It replaced the timber structure that had been in place since the summer of 1848, and was one of a number of unavoidable improvements the GNR had to carry out in the 1880s. (Boots Cash Chemists Real Photograph Series postcard/Author's collection)

St Ann's Well station on the Nottingham Suburban Railway worked by the GNR was built with full facilities for passengers and goods, as were the other two stations on the three and a half mile (5.6km) long line. It never really stimulated the creation of a new Nottingham suburb as hoped. (Official photograph/Author's collection)

Cross Keys swing bridge at Sutton Bridge was erected in 1897, the last of three replacement bridges at this location crossing the River Nene. On this section of the M&GN Joint line, the MR was responsible for the signalling, and that company's fine semaphores are on show here. (Commercial postcard/ Author's collection)

The new line opened in the summer of 1890 and became a joint undertaking with the L&YR four years later.

In 1882 the Midland & Eastern Railway (M&ER) (see page 31) had amalgamated with other small East Anglian lines to form the Eastern & Midlands Railway (E&MR). By the end of the decade that company's network stretched from Bourne (formerly Bourn) through Spalding to Sutton Bridge and from Peterborough through Wisbeach to Sutton Bridge, with a line from there through Lynn to Melton Constable, where branches radiated to Norwich, Cromer and Great Yarmouth via North Walsham. From June 1889 the network was divided into two sections, that west of Lynn controlled

by a joint committee of the MR and GNR, with the remainder in the hands of receivers for the M&ER. In the same year, authority was secured for the link that had first been proposed almost twenty-five years previously. This was the connection between Bourne and Saxby on the MR's Leicester (Syston)–Peterborough line that since 1880 had become part of the MR's main line between Nottingham and Glendon Junction just north of Kettering. Then in June 1893 the Royal Assent was granted for the creation of the Midland & Great Northern Joint Railway (M&GN Joint) with powers to transfer all former E&MR land, plant and equipment and personnel to the new organisation. In the same month the

Bourne–Saxby line was opened for goods traffic, with a passenger services following in May 1894.

The MS&LR 'London Extension'

Charles Grinling, in *The History of the Great Northern Railway 1845–1895* (Methuen & Co, 1898) refers more than once to what he believed was the GNR's mistaken policy of appeasement with rivals and the wasting of resources on joint undertakings that could have been better used on other projects. In regard to the GNR's relationship with the MS&LR over whose lines the former was able to reach Manchester and via the CLC further into Lancashire, Grinling's opinion was that the GNR should have promoted and built its own line into Manchester. That was obviously the view of a believer in the economics of competition that, ironically, was the reason the MS&LR promoted its 'London Extension' in this period, to which Grinling was opposed.

As a prelude to the story of this line, it has to be recorded that in 1881, the Fifty Year Agreement of 1858 between the GNR and MS&LR had been stripped of one particular clause that a Railway Commission of that year had deemed too protectionist and against the public interest. Although this did little to affect the successful operation of the partners' London–Manchester service, it had made the GNR Board nervous about a further weakening of the relationship, especially with the ambitious Sir Edward Watkin in control of the MS&LR.

The *status quo* was uneasily maintained until the very end of the decade, by which time Watkin was not only chairman of the MS&LR but also the MetR. In 1889 both those companies put Bills before Parliament that the GNR – and others – believed was an attempt by Watkin to create a new route so that MS&LR trains could reach London. (The first serious schemes floated in the 1870s have been referred to in the previous chapter.) The 1889 MS&LR Bill was for a line from Beighton, just outside Sheffield,

southwards to join the GNR's Leen Valley line at Annesley, put forward as a way for the MS&LR to reach the Nottinghamshire coalfields. The justification for the 1889 MetR Bill was less convincing. Having already gained powers to extend to Aylesbury and link up with the Aylesbury & Buckingham Railway there, the MetR's Bill was for a new line from Quainton Road station on that line to Moreton Pinkney on the East & West Railway so that via that line to Stratford-on-Avon, and onwards to Broom over another company's line, a new route from London to Worcester could be created. The GNR believed the stated aim of reaching Worcester was a ruse and the real intent was ultimately to form a new London–Manchester route. History proved this analysis was correct, but in 1889, when the GNR in communication with the MS&LR specifically voiced its concerns, this was denied.

The Bill for the Beighton extension was passed, but the MetR's 'Worcester & Broom Railway' failed to secure its Act. Very soon afterwards Watkin's pretence of the Worcester project was completely discarded and the MS&LR announced plans to extend from Annesley to Quainton Road. The GNR was invited to take part in the new scheme but, needless to say, it declined the offer and its opposition combined with that of both the two other main north–south trunk railway companies, namely the MR and LNWR, succeeded in defeating the 'London Extension Bill' in the Parliamentary session of 1891. Determined to present the Bill again (with slight detail changes), the MS&LR immediately reopened negotiations with the GNR. The concessions offered were apparently enough this time for the GNR to withdraw its opposition to the new Bill. Running powers were to be granted to the GNR from Nottingham to all parts of the MS&LR network west of Sheffield, including the CLC lines. At Nottingham, the GNR would share in the building and running of a new joint station. In return, the GNR granted the MS&LR running powers onto

King's Cross station and its environs as they appeared at the end of the nineteenth century when the MS&LR was poised to reach the capital from Annesley, Nottinghamshire. (E. Pouteau postcard/Author's collection)

its lines in the West Riding. In October 1892 MS&LR trains began to run along the completed Beighton extension into the GNR's Nottingham London Road station, and at the end of March the following year the MS&LR's 'London Extension Act' received the Royal Assent. After thirty-five years, the GNR and MS&LR 'Fifty Year Agreement' had effectively, though not legally, come to an end.

Waiting to take over a King's Cross-Manchester (London Road) express from its GNR engine at Grantham, is MS&LR 4-4-0 no.694. Photographed when brand new in 1895, the MS&LR's own line to London was already under construction signalling the end of a successful joint venture. (Locomotive Publishing Co./Author's collection)

END OF THE VICTORIAN ERA

The end of the Victorian era witnessed the retirement of four men who had done more than any others to create the look and to shape the operation of the GNR since the end of the 1860s. They were Francis P. Cockshott, Superintendent of the Line 1865–1895; Patrick Stirling, Locomotive Engineer 1866–1895; Richard Johnson, Chief Engineer 1861–1896, and Henry Oakley, General Manager 1870–1898.

Johnson had the longest association with the GNR. He had started as an employee of one of the contractors building the 'Loop' line back in the 1840s and worked his way up to become Chief Engineer in 1861, holding that position for the next 35 years. He was responsible for designing, building,

The 1852 Warren Truss bridges over the Trent Dyke, just north of Newark, were just some of the numerous structures Richard Johnson as Chief Engineer was responsible for. Repairs had proved insufficient so in 1889 Handyside & Co. of Derby was given the task of replacing them with two new steel Whipple Murphy designs. This photograph was taken in August 1889 just before the down spans were exchanged. (Official photograph/Author's collection)

maintaining and repairing all sorts of structures, as well as supervising the surveying and construction of completely new lines.

Oakley's career was almost as long having been the company's Accountant in 1857 and 1858 and then its Secretary between 1858 and 1870.

Impressive though this record of service was, however, these men perhaps allowed the company to cling on a little too long to tried and tested ways in all areas of its activities firmly centred on economy.

Speed v comfort

Also marking the end of an era was the celebrated 'Race to Aberdeen' that broke out in 1895 between the East Coast and West Coast railway partners. As with the race of 1888, it was exciting, but when viewed objectively it was only a piece of theatre, a brief distraction in a period when railway companies were progressively providing their travellers with better and more comfortable facilities.

The race had been triggered in 1894 when the best journey time between London and Aberdeen over the East Coast route was reduced from 12hr 15min to 11hr 35min. This bettered the West Coast partners' times for their equivalent overnight Anglo–Scottish service and for the summer of 1895 they managed to trim their schedule to 11hr 40min.

This photograph has been reproduced before (with various inaccurate captions) but is included here to show the changing scene on the GNR at the time of the 1895 'Race to Aberdeen'. Stirling '8ft single' No. 221 is about to take out an afternoon express comprising six-wheeled carriages. As the King's Cross station clock shows 1.25pm, it is probably the 1.30pm to Leeds and Bradford. In stark contrast to the six-wheeled stock and a glimpse of things to come, is the East Coast Joint Stock (ECJS) Dining Saloon No. 223 on the left, built at Doncaster in 1894 with clerestory roof and two four-wheeled bogies. (F. Moore's Railway Photographs/Author's collection)

The East Coast responded by reducing their time to 11hr 20min. As the London to Edinburgh section of the journey was then completed faster than the times set by the 'gentleman's agreement' of 1888, the West Coast partners cried foul and so the race was on. It continued through July and into August, the last sprint by the East Coast partners taking place on 21 August when Edinburgh was reached from London King's Cross in 6hrs 19mins and Aberdeen in just 8hrs 40mins. That was enough for them but on the following day the West Coast made one last dash through the night with just three carriages, reaching Aberdeen from London Euston in 8hrs 32mins.

In purely commercial terms racing with a few lightly laden carriages was not the best way to retain and grow Anglo–Scottish passenger traffic. For both the West and East Coast partners the way forward was to continue to improve passenger facilities. As noted in the previous chapter, this had started with coaches carried on two bogies of either four or six wheels each. In July 1893, four new first class and four new third class dining cars, along with eight new third class corridor coaches had gone into service on afternoon East Coast Anglo–Scottish trains, all with gangway connections between the vehicles. This use of dining cars in ECJS trains eventually lead to the withdrawal of the refreshment breaks at York that had become such a feature of these services for many years. More dining saloons were built at Doncaster Works the following year, 52ft 6in (16m) long vehicles with clerestory roofs. These were soon made to look very modest when 64ft (19.5m) monsters appeared two years later, carried on two six-wheel bogies, with a number of composite corridor (i.e. with both first and third class seats) and all third class corridor carriages constructed at the same time.

There were two significant and very progressive features about these vehicles. The first was the use of Pullman pattern gangway connections that eventually became standard on ECJS and later GNR carriages and was perpetuated through subsequent LNER coach designs. The second was the use of automatic couplers made by the Gould Coupler Co. of Depew, New York. Ultimately the GNR settled on what were termed 'buckeye' automatic couplings, although these and Gould's designs shared similar characteristics as they were capable of being joined. (Buckeye couplers as with Pullman gangways became another LNER standard.)

More power

In the summer of 1893, Oakley had written to Stirling saying '…We must have more power or run more slowly. We cannot contemplate the latter as we have won our prestige by our good and speedy service. The only course is to increase our power. What can you do in this direction?' As an interim measure in time for the new summer timetable of 1894, Stirling's ban on double-heading express trains was rescinded but his considered response to the need for more powerful locomotives was perhaps inevitable for a seventy-four year old engineer. He sought to improve his '8ft single' design rather than replace it with a completely new one and at the end of the year an 'upgraded' version appeared from Doncaster Works. Various vital statistics were changed but despite these alterations, the overall 1870s design remained unchanged. Nevertheless, Stirling was still held in high regard and convinced the Board that the upgraded engine was answering the need for 'more power'. Approval was granted for a further five engines and they were completed between January and April 1895. But just as Sturrock's championing of steam tenders thirty years earlier had caused the Board to question the judgment of its locomotive engineer, so Stirling's faith in his iconic single wheeler placed the Board in a dilemma. Stirling had only hinted at retiring, and as there was no obvious successor within

Almost certainly the down 'Special Scotch Express' made up entirely of new clerestory, bogie carriages heading through Harringay in 1898 with two Stirling '8ft singles' in charge. The leading engine is either No. 1008 or No. 1003, the latter being involved in the accident at Little Bytham on 7 March 1896.
(Dr Budden/R.S. Carpenter collection)

Hauling the 10am 'Flying Scotchman' up the 1 in 107 gradient towards Holloway is another pair of '8ft singles', the leading engine No. 1007 completed at Doncaster Works in March 1895. The photograph was taken sometime between then and 1900 when the Caledonian Down signalbox seen on the right was abolished.
(Author's collection)

the company, a select group of Board members started to look around discreetly for a future replacement. After careful consideration, H.A. Ivatt, Locomotive Engineer of the Great Southern & Western Railway of Ireland, was confirmed as Stirling's replacement at a Board meeting on 1 November 1895 attended by Stirling himself. A few days later on the night of 10 November, one of the new '8ft singles' – No. 1006 – was involved in high-speed derailment at St Neots. The accident in which two passengers were killed was caused by a rail breaking under the train partly due to the increased axle load of the engine. Stirling died the following day.

New brooms

The accident had been caused by the breakage of an old worn rail that had been inadvertently refitted into a section of the main line. Another accident at Little Bytham on 7 March 1896 was due to a speeding express train distorting the track and becoming derailed as a result. What both accidents revealed was that the GNR had taken economy almost to the point of being unsafe. The recycling of old rails was obviously a common occurrence such that no one had questioned the fitness of the rail reused at St Neots. At Little Bytham, a temporary speed restriction over a recently repaired section of track had been prematurely lifted so as not to delay traffic.

An illustration of just how poor GNR main line track was in the first half of the 1890s. Confidently spinning along through Hornsey with a down express is brand new Stirling 2-2-2 No. 872 built the year this photograph was taken – 1892. (Locomotive & General Railway Photographs 22199/ Author's collection)

A gang at the north end of Essendine station posed for an official photograph to illustrate the method of ensuring the post 1896 main line remained in perfect alignment. (Peterborough Museum Ce12)

Stirling 2-4-0 No. 708 emerges from Hadley Wood South Tunnel with a London-bound train as a couple of men work on a replacement sleeper. A metal frame has ensured the correct gauge between the two chairs is maintained as they hand drill the holes for the spikes that will fasten the chairs to the sleeper. (Author's collection)

The signalbox at Lolham, seven miles north of Peterborough, was opened in September 1898 as part of the work that had seen the completion of the down slow line between Helpston and Tallington. With the addition of this alongside the existing main lines and the up slow line, the GNR felt it necessary to provide a footbridge to straddle all four tracks. (Commercial postcard 4.12.1910/Author's collection)

Consequently, one of the first tasks undertaken by H.A. Ivatt after he took charge as Locomotive Engineer at the beginning of March 1896 was to assess the fitness of the permanent way to support the planned more powerful locomotives and heavier rolling stock. The new man almost certainly revealed what many already suspected, and very quickly a programme of relaying the main line with new steel rails and chairs was begun.

This decision was made in the same year as the appointment of two other new officers, both directly responsible for the physical operation of the railway. The new Superintendent of the Line was J. Alexander, starting his job at the beginning of January 1896 after his former boss Cockshott had retired. The new Chief Engineer was Alexander Ross, who had been lured away from the same position with MS&LR having been, until his appointment with the GNR in December 1896, intimately involved with that company's 'London Extension'.

The evidence that a new Locomotive Engineer was in charge at Doncaster came very quickly. Within months of his appointment, Ivatt had had a new design of boiler made and fitted to Stirling '8ft single' No. 93. It sported a large steam dome, and coming so soon after thirty years of Stirling's straightback design, must have been a shock to staff and passengers alike. The engine emerged from Doncaster Works in June 1896. Another member of the class, No. 776, was the next to receive a new boiler, but with the diameter of the dome reduced by six inches (15cm). Six other locomotives were similarly dealt but the remainder of the class continued to run in the form Stirling left them, valiantly soldiering on with increasingly heavy trains.

A down express at Hitchin South headed by Stirling '8ft single' No. 95 sporting its replacement Ivatt domed boiler and new style of smokebox door and cab, fitted in the summer of 1897. On the adjacent up slow line, Stirling 0-6-0 No. 748 of 1882 gleams in comparison to the attached travel-worn 'Goods Break' No. 10864. (F. Moore's Railway Photographs 2633/Author's collection)

Although Ivatt respected the work of his predecessor and understood in what affection Stirling's engines were held, in the interests of efficiency he could, nevertheless, produce travesties such as this. In 1901, No. 548 was fitted experimentally with a spark arrester that required an extension to the smokebox. Neither the new aesthetic nor the smoke arrester were a success. (Author's collection)

The first engine of Ivatt's own design appeared at the end of 1896. Its 4-4-0 wheel arrangement had not been used before by the company, although in essence the locomotive was a modest enlargement of a 2-4-0 engine, that wheel arrangement having been used by the GNR since the 1840s. As well as a domed boiler, the 4-4-0 had a modified Stirling cab with an extension over the footplate. It was a cautious start, but early in 1897 plans were approved for a 4-4-2 express passenger locomotive and a little later drawings were prepared for a tank engine with the same wheel arrangement. The latter was the first to emerge from Doncaster Works in February 1898 and sent to work over the difficult West Riding lines. Then in May the tender engine with that wheel arrangement appeared, causing more of a stir because it was the first 'Atlantic' tender engine in the country.

With hindsight it was the 'Atlantic' that paved the way to the GNR's – and ultimately the LNER's – 'big engine policy', but in 1898 that progression had not yet become apparent, and in October that year a new single wheeler 4-2-2 express passenger engine took to road. Both this locomotive and the 'Atlantic' were viewed as prototypes and went through a period of evaluation before a further ten of the latter and ten more 4-2-2s with slight modifications were built in 1900, and one additional 4-2-2 put to work the following year.

Although a post-First World War photograph, this scene at Ganwick just south of Potters Bar Tunnel neatly illustrates the evolution of locomotive design in the 1890s. The leading engine No. 883 was one of Stirling's 2-4-0s of 1892 fitted with a new Ivatt domed boiler in 1905. The train engine is No. 1388 of 1903, Ivatt's updating of Stirling's 2-4-0 design by the addition of a leading bogie and larger boiler. (Gordon Tidey/Author's collection)

One of Ivatt's sixth batch of 4-4-0s, No. 1331 of 1898 photographed backing onto its train at Lincoln station. (Author's collection)

Ivatt 4-4-2T No. 1020 of 1899 at Bradford Exchange station. Although owned by the L&YR, the GNR also used the station, dedicated platforms for the use of the company being part of the enlargement completed there between 1885 and 1888. (Author's collection)

Ivatt's pioneering 4-4-2 'Atlantic' No. 990 in original condition but photographed at Ganwick with an up train shortly after being named *Henry Oakley* in June 1900. The term 'Atlantic' had been coined in 1896 in the USA for engines with the 4-4-2 wheel arrangement that worked the expresses between Camden and Atlantic City. The GNR locomotive class also earned the nickname 'Klondyke' as the North American gold rush had been in the headlines at the time of its construction. (Dr. Sellon/Author's collection)

This photograph at the south end of Grantham station was taken sometime between 1901 when Ivatt 4-2-2 No. 264 was outshopped from Doncaster Works, and March 1903 when Stirling '8ft single' No. 771 was scrapped. Whilst the Stirling engine pulls away southwards with its train, No. 264 waits to take over the next up service. (Rev. Thomas Bernard Parley/Author's collection)

The GNR's first water troughs for replenishing locomotive tenders without stopping were laid in 1900 at Muskham, just over two miles (3.2km) north of Newark, and Werrington, just over three miles (4.8km) north of Peterborough. Werrington troughs seen here were 800yds (731.5m) long and the depth of water in them just 4½in (11.4cm). 'Klondyke' No. 986 is hauling an up express. (Locomotive Publishing Co. 1329/Author's collection)

London suburban improvements

After the considerable expenditure on suburban improvements in the 1880s, the GNR hoped for some relief from the seemingly endless growth in commuter traffic, when negotiations were entered into with the Great Northern & City that proposed to build an underground line from Finsbury Park into the city. The intention was to make a junction with the main line at Finsbury Park so as to allow GNR trains to use the new line. Even for the cautious and aging GNR management of the early 1890s, progress was slow, and with delays and overcrowding reflecting badly on the company they had no alternative but to upgrade their existing facilities yet again. King's Cross Suburban station was remodelled, involving the easing of the Hotel Curve through that station, and the provision

of extra platforms covered by a new roof. This was completed in the spring of 1895. At the same time New Barnet station was extensively rebuilt with a new overhead booking office similar to those at Harringay, Hadley Wood and New Southgate. The new facilities were brought into use in September 1895.

Between Holloway and Wood Green an additional slow line for north-bound trains was created and track layouts rearranged at those stations and at Finsbury Park, Harringay, and Hornsey. At the latter a new island platform was created, along with the erection of a new booking hall suspended over the tracks, all brought into use in November 1899. At Holloway, the down platform was re-sited and the new buildings on it protected by a generous canopy. At Harringay the changes were not so dramatic but as at Holloway

New Barnet station after the rebuilding of 1895. A survivor from an earlier upgrade in 1876–7 is the up platform canopy seen to the right of the train.
(Commercial postcard/Author's collection)

Standing ready at King's Cross with its destination board in place, Ivatt 4-4-2T No. 1546 was one of a batch of ten of this class of engine built at Doncaster in 1907 to provide motive power for London suburban services.
(F. Moore Railway Photographs 2642/Author's collection)

The south end of Harringay station photographed in 1903 after the final alterations and the erection of the down line signalbox (on the right). The other signalbox visible for controlling up trains was brought into use almost twenty years earlier. On the left is Stirling 0-4-4 well tank No. 531 of 1875 with a London-bound suburban train, the four-wheeled, third class carriage being of the same vintage. (P. Rutherford/Author's collection)

Ivatt 4-4-2 tank No. 1505 built in 1899 was the fiftieth member of this class of locomotive and the fifth fitted with condensing apparatus from new to work the London suburban services between Moorgate on the Metropolitan Railway's underground system and the GNR's stations north of King's Cross and as far as Hatfield. When only a few years old the engine was photographed waiting to leave King's Cross station. (Locomotive & General Railway Photographs/Author's collection)

and Hornsey (and previously at New Southgate and New Barnet), extensive re-signalling also had to be undertaken, this and Holloway station being completed by the summer of 1901.

Goods growth

In the last years of the nineteenth century, goods and mineral traffic had continued to grow, despite the disquiet amongst railway companies about the new classification for 'merchandise traffic' that legislation had obliged them to implement in 1893. This acted as a spur to improve the efficiency and reduce the costs of handling goods. In

London, the GNR enlarged its Farringdon Street Goods Depot in 1895, and the goods yard at King's Cross was reorganised four years later. The Farringdon Street work included the erection of an impressive four storey building on the corner of Turnmill Street and Clerkenwell Green (later Clerkenwell Road) for both goods storage and the stabling of up to 200 horses used for shunting wagons and hauling delivery vans and carts. On the outskirts of Leeds, a new goods station was opened at Hunslet in July 1899. Although the connecting line from a junction at Beeston was only four and a half miles (7.2km)

Improvements on the High Barnet and Edgware branches in the last years of the nineteenth century included the provision of an island platform at Highgate, seen in this Edwardian view. (F.E. Clarke photographer/ Commercial postcard/ Author's collection)

Providing the motive power for this mixed goods train approaching Hatfield on the up slow line in the first decade of the twentieth century, is Stirling 2-4-0 No. 214 of 1889. (F. Moore Railway Photographs 2642/Author's collection)

For both Stirling and Ivatt, the design favoured for shunting yards and working short distance goods trains was the 0-6-0 saddle tank, two examples of which are seen here. No. 693 on the left was designed by Stirling and built at Doncaster Works in 1883, and on the right is Ivatt's updated version, No. 1265, constructed in 1902. (Author's collection)

A shortage of engines, with Doncaster and other British locomotive works too busy to satisfy the demand in the last years of the nineteenth century, led the GNR (and other companies) to patronise firms in the United States of America. This was one of twenty 'Yankees', all but one supplied as kits of parts to the GNR by Baldwin's Locomotive Works, Philadelphia in 1899. It was assembled at Ardsley (Leeds) and was photographed at Bradford in 1906 with a characteristically GNR smokebox door. It was scrapped in March 1909. (Real Photographs 16285/Author's collection)

long, it involved the erection of a costly swing bridge over the Aire & Calder Navigation. In 1897 a large new engine shed was brought into use at Colwick Yard, and a few years later, extra sidings were laid so that the yard could deal with 6,000 ten-ton wagons. At the other end of the 'coal chain', a new engine shed for forty locomotives was built at Ferme Park Yard and brought into use in the summer of 1899.

The Great Central Railway

Work had started on the MS&LR's extension to London at the end of 1894. Although the GNR had agreed to part finance and run a new central station in Nottingham, it had not formally become involved in the planning until November 1895. As a result, excavation of the station site and construction of the buildings commenced some months after work on the rest of the line was well advanced. When the station finally opened on the

monarch's birthday – 24 May 1900 – to be christened Victoria in her honour, it was a fitting and magnificent monument to mark the end of Britain's great century of railway building.

By then, the MS&LR had renamed itself (in August 1897) the Great Central Railway (GCR) and coal trains had been running over the new main line to London for a little over two years, with passenger services to Marylebone station inaugurated on 15 March 1899. The GNR's junctions with the GCR north and south of Nottingham had also been ready to take passenger trains at that time. These new connections allowed the GNR to significantly improve its local services in two ways. The first obvious advantage was the use of a new station with brand new facilities in the centre of the city (that status conferred in June 1897). The second advantage was the ability to operate trains through the new central station instead of having to run them into and

A photograph of the south end of Nottingham Victoria station nearing completion in the spring of 1900.
(F. Moore's Photographs/ Author's collection)

Basford & Bulwell station looking almost due east. The line curving away sharply to the left linked with the GCR main line at Bulwell South Junction. Adjacent to the 1898 signalbox and a little beyond, the lines split in three directions, double track continuing as part of the original GNR's 'Derbyshire & Staffordshire Extension' route to Colwick Yard, with up and down single lines looping south to join the GCR main line at Bagthorpe Junction. (Official photograph/Author's collection)

then out of the London Road (Low Level) terminus. As to main line services, the advantages were not so great. To compete directly with the new GCR's London–Manchester trains all with dining car facilities, the GNR diverted the former services run in conjunction with the MS&LR, away from Retford and through Grantham and Nottingham Victoria to Manchester Central, the CLC terminus in that city. Apart from giving Nottingham a new express service, Manchester passengers had to be satisfied with a journey a quarter of an hour slower than previously.

Arguably the most remunerative outcome for the GNR in gaining running powers north of Nottingham over the new GCR main line, was in the goods and minerals department. As soon as the MS&LR's London Extension had received its Act, the GNR drew up plans for a large new goods warehouse in Manchester, Deansgate. With the support of the city's corporation, an Act was secured in 1895 and nine acres (3.6ha)

adjacent to Manchester Central Station was cleared of houses, shops, offices, and other buildings to make way for the new facility. The yard was brought into use on 1 July 1898, with completion of the warehouse achieved at the beginning of July 1899. Unfortunately, the GNR and GCR were in dispute at Grimsby at the time and the GCR was less than co-operative about dealing with the GNR's Manchester trains. This prompted the GNR to make hasty arrangements with the MR and a new junction was brought into use between their two routes in the Erewash Valley, enabling the GNR to run its trains between Manchester and Colwick Yard over MR lines. It was not until the summer of 1900 that the GCR and GNR resolved their dispute.

Before the Grimsby spat and during the period when the MS&LR was feeling grateful to the GNR for withdrawing its opposition to the London Extension plans, the GNR had been able to extract one further concession from the MS&LR. Since the beginning of the 1890s, the GNR

The GNR's warehouse at Deansgate, Manchester under construction. One of the steel beams is clearly marked 'E.C. & J. Keay Ltd, Darlaston', the Black Country firm that went on to fabricate the steel work for the dome of the Victoria & Albert Museum in London as well as the metalwork for the Great Western Railway's new station at Birmingham, Snow Hill. (Great Northern Railway Society/P092394)

had looked to extend its Leen Valley line further north to where new deep coal mines were being sunk, and in June 1892 it had secured an Act for that extension. The original plan included a tunnel through the Robin Hood Hills near Annesley, but as the MS&LR was on the point of opening its own line at that location on its Beighton Extension, it was persuaded to allow the GNR to use its tunnel. As a result, the GNR's extension was separated from its existing Leen Valley line by a section of GCR main line. The extension branched off that main line just north of Annesley tunnel heading northwards through some difficult terrain and opening in various stages until it reached Shirebrook in November 1900. A little further north it then made a connection with the Lancashire, Derbyshire & East Coast Railway (LD&ECR) at Langwith

Junction, completed for the end of May the following year.

The LD&ECR had its origins back in 1887 when promoters around Shirebrook – the Dukeries area of Nottinghamshire – had secured an Act to build a line from a junction with the GNR main line at North Muskham, three miles (4.8km) north of Newark, to Ollerton. The GNR was approached to help build and then operate the new route but it declined. Within a few years the promoters refocused on a far more ambitious scheme to build a line from the Manchester Ship Canal, through Ollerton and Lincoln to a new coal port at Sutton-on-Sea on the Lincolnshire coast. Surprisingly MPs were persuaded of the advantages of this new route and sanctioned the 200 mile (322km) long railway in 1891. Financing the scheme proved very difficult, however, the main

The GNR's stone-faced station at Sutton-in-Ashfield on its Leen Valley Extension was officially opened at the beginning of April 1898. (Official photograph/Author's collection)

Summit signalbox at Kirkby-in-Ashfield opened in April 1898 on the first section of the GNR's Leen Valley Extension to reach Skegby that year. (Author's collection)

Photographed in about 1895 is the LD&ECR's bridge over the GNR main line just south of that company's 1852 Tuxford station away in the distance. This will be the location of Dukeries Junction station, the photographer standing on the site of the GNR's down platforms with the up one directly opposite. The station was brought into use in June 1897. (Official photograph/Author's collection)

backer being the GER who saw potential in the central section of the line through Lincoln, where connections could be made with the GN&GE Joint line. But it was not interested in the route west of Chesterfield and east from Lincoln and as a result, those sections were never built. Neither was the Newark & Ollerton Railway that had become part of the LD&ECR's portfolio. When the line between Chesterfield and Lincoln opened in March 1897 a connection with the GNR was brought into use at Tuxford, where exchange sidings were provided next to the main line. Where the two lines crossed, a two level interchange station was opened in June that year and named Dukeries Junction with the hope it might soon be dealing with visitors to the ancient Sherwood Forest and Dukeries estates.

EDWARDIAN SPLENDOUR

The MS&LR's push to reach London at the end of the nineteenth century could be seen as the final flourish of Victorian inter-company rivalry and competition. A few years later there was an example of co-operation that harked back to the period in the 1840s when amalgamations were creating powerful companies such as the MR, LNWR and L&YR. Aware that the 'Fifty Year Agreement' between the GNR and the GCR was close to its official end, during a conversation between the two companies' General Managers in 1907 a merger was discussed. In June 1908, the GER became involved and another agreement was drawn up between all three companies. Conscious this new larger organisation would undoubtedly be opposed by other railways, the MR

The south end of York station with a line-up of trains from all the companies that might have been amalgamated within months of this photograph having been taken in 1907/8. From left to right the locomotives are NER, MR, NER, GNR (with a MR engine and train behind), GER, and GNR. The GNR engine in front of the MR train is Ivatt 4-4-0 No. 1332 of 1898, probably waiting to take over from NER 4-6-0 No. 2114 (built in 1901) in the adjacent platform with what looks to be ECJS. (Locomotive Publishing Co./Author's collection)

was approached to join the merger but declined. In 1909 an amalgamation Bill was submitted to Parliament and, as President of the Board of Trade, Winston Churchill confirmed the Government's guarded support. A special Parliamentary Committee was set up to consider the Bill but when it was obvious MPs were becoming distracted by broader national questions about the merits of competition versus nationalisation, the GNR, GCR and GER withdrew their Bill.

Towards greater efficiencies

New ideas were also taking hold in Doncaster Works during the Edwardian era and in July 1902 the GNR's first multiple cylinder engine made its appearance, a four cylinder 'Klondyke' – No. 271. Then five months later in December everyone was amazed by the appearance of 'Atlantic' No. 251 with a boiler diameter of 5ft 6in (1.67m) and the widest firebox to be seen on a British locomotive at the time. No. 271 was built with the aim of improving the efficiency and reducing the running costs of express locomotives, but No. 251 was very obviously and simply a response to the need for 'more power'.

The performance of the two locomotives was carefully assessed as ideas also turned to compounding – using the steam generated in a locomotive's boiler twice through high and low pressure cylinders before it was exhausted to the atmosphere. Between 1904 and 1907 trials were carried out between a standard engine and a couple of four-cylinder compound 'Atlantics'

The 1905 Vulcan Foundry four cylinder compound 'Atlantic' at King's Cross with one of Ivatt's 2-4-0 of 1897 – No. 1065 – resting alongside. (W. Hopkins-Brown/Author's collection)

Another photograph that has been reproduced before but perhaps not from a print in which such care was taken to 'burn' in the exhaust from the locomotive. Only the third 'Atlantic' to be built with a large boiler, No. 273 of 1904 hauling the 10am Bradford–King's Cross is seen picking up water from the troughs laid near Scrooby in 1902. (Author's collection)

Ivatt 'Atlantic' No. 1441 of 1908 pulls out of King's Cross station, its size emphasised by its train of what were even then considered old-fashioned six-wheeled carriages. The somersault signal in the 'off' position is signalling the train out of No. 1 departure platform to the down main No. 2 line. (Rex Conway collection)

The line-up outside King's Cross 'Top Shed', a photograph probably taken to show off Ivatt 'Atlantic' No. 1414 built in 1906. Alongside is 2-4-0 No. 864, intriguingly carrying the headboard 'Burton' used by engines working through from the GNR's 'Derbyshire & Staffordshire Extension' lines to Burton-upon-Trent. (Author's collection)

with large boilers all built at Doncaster, and another four-cylinder compound engine with the same wheel arrangement supplied by the Vulcan Foundry in Newton-le-Willows in 1905. All these experiments proved inconclusive and by 1908 eighty, two-cylinder 'simple' large boilered 'Atlantics' had been turned out from Doncaster Works and, although not completely as economical as the Board would have liked, proved more than capable of hauling heavier passenger trains.

Whilst Ivatt's large boilered 'Atlantics' took the strain of express work, in complete contrast for country branches the GNR experimented with 'rail motor cars'. These were diminutive steam locomotives permanently attached to a single carriage and in 1906 six were put to work operating services between Grimsby and Louth, over the Mablethorpe 'loop', on the Finchley–Edgware section of the High Barnet branch and between Ossett and Batley. Later, two cars were moved to work between Hitchin, Letchworth and Baldock, a temporary station having

opened at Letchworth to serve the developers of the 'Garden City' there in April 1904. The West Riding rail motor car services ended in 1908 with the vehicles transferred to Lincolnshire, where services there and in Hertfordshire continued until 1917.

Efficiencies were also looked for in the handling of goods and mineral traffic in this period. Between 1901 and 1909, fifty-five 0-8-0 tender engines were built, most put to work on coal trains between the Nottinghamshire & Derbyshire coalfield and London, as well as hauling trains carrying the increasing output of bricks from the works immediately south of Peterborough. In the same period the GNR was also investing in goods trains fitted with continuous brakes that could be run at almost express passenger speeds for the transport of more valuable and perishable commodities. Between 1900 and 1903, 250 vans all 'piped' – i.e. fitted for automatic vacuum brake use – were built especially for these services, and others were converted. Fast goods trains were then able to work regularly over the main line to and

A little group pose in front of Doncaster-built rail motor car No. 1 at Finchley, Church End station in 1909 after it had been transferred from working in Lincolnshire. The carriage was the first of Gresley's designs as the company's new Carriage & Wagon Superintendent. (WHS Kingsway Real Photo Series postcard/Author's collection)

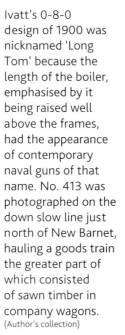

Ivatt's 0-8-0 design of 1900 was nicknamed 'Long Tom' because the length of the boiler, emphasised by it being raised well above the frames, had the appearance of contemporary naval guns of that name. No. 413 was photographed on the down slow line just north of New Barnet, hauling a goods train the greater part of which consisted of sawn timber in company wagons. (Author's collection)

'Long Toms' and an impressive line up of Ivatt 4-4-0s at Peterborough's New England running shed in the first decade of the twentieth century. In 1905 it was recorded that of the forty 'Long Toms' at work, twenty-six were allocated to Peterborough, eleven to Colwick and three to Doncaster. (C. Laundy/Author's collection)

Making a stiring sight with a south-bound express from York, immaculately turned out superheated Ivatt 'Atlantic' No. 1456 of 1910 hauls a train through the race course station. (Coltas collection)

from Manchester, Liverpool, Nottingham, Derby, Halifax, Edinburgh and Glasgow, the best service between London and Manchester Deansgate, for example, taking just 5hr 50min. In 1908 Ivatt put into service a fleet of fifteen powerful 0-6-0s with 5ft 8in (1.72m) diameter wheels especially for these services.

One of Ivatt's last experiments with locomotive design was the superheating of steam before it entered the cylinders. In later years this was to become a standard feature on the majority of locomotives to improve the overall efficiency of the machine, but in this period it was also considered as a way of reducing boiler maintenance by enabling boilers to produce steam at a lower pressure. Satisfied with the results of a superheated 0-8-0 and 'Klondyke', Ivatt had superheaters fitted to the final batch of ten large boilered 'Atlantics' built in 1910, their working pressures reduced

from 175psi to 150psi and the cylinder diameter increased.

Carriages for a new age

None of the experiments mentioned above were unique to the GNR. Other locomotive engineers were similarly interested in compounding and superheating and it showed that Ivatt was more open to outside influences than Stirling ever was. This willingness to embrace new ideas soon became evident in Ivatt's successor – Herbert Nigel Gresley. Unlike all previous GNR Locomotive Engineers, Gresley had already been employed by the company for a few months short of seven years as its Carriage & Wagon Superintendent. During that time he had certainly made an impression, because just as Ivatt had caused a stir by adding a dome to GNR locomotive boilers, so Gresley had turned heads by removing the clerestory roof on Doncaster-built carriages.

The 1.05pm Sheffield–King's Cross express made up of Gresley's new 'Sheffield stock' of 1906 photographed near Godley on the GCR section of the journey, hauled by Stirling 2-4-0 No. 993 of 1894 with its new Ivatt domed boiler of 1904. The GNR dynasty in one train! (E. Pouteau/Author's collection)

His first main line design was a corridor composite completed at Doncaster in December 1905 with a distinctive elliptical roof with curved ends. Designed and built within a few months of this coach was a set of four carriages for the King's Cross–Manchester services, each vehicle with the new roof style and carried on two, four-wheel bogies. At this time the GNR still felt compelled to compete with GCR trains to and from London Marylebone and only the previous year had put on a late afternoon service that ran non-stop to Sheffield in 2hr 50min and onwards to reach Manchester in 4hr. The mid-afternoon train in the opposite direction was a little slower but still included a non-stop Sheffield–London run.

By the time Gresley's carriages formed the train a stop had been inserted in the southbound run but this did not detract from management's view that it was still a prestige service. Gresley's new 'Sheffield Stock' as good as created the template for all subsequent GNR, ECJS and LNER carriages until the 1940s. So supportive was the Board of Gresley's new features that in 1907 it insisted against the wishes of the NER, the most important partner in the Anglo–Scottish services, that all future coaches for those trains should be built to the new Doncaster pattern.

As well as new designs, Gresley also contributed to the long GNR tradition of recycling equipment, and to extract a little more life from the stock of old six-wheeled

A train of NER straight-sided stock built in 1903 for the King's Cross–Newcastle services, heading south at Walton just north of Peterborough behind 'Klondyke' No. 984 of 1900. When the NER built similar stock as its contribution to ECJS, *Railway Magazine* of December 1906 described them as looking as though they had '…been built in an American lumber yard…'. (C. Laundy/Author's collection)

Carriages built to Gresley's new designs after 1907 gradually changed the look of GNR expresses such as this one, climbing out of King's Cross through Holloway & Caledonian Road station behind Ivatt 'Atlantic' No. 281 of 1905. The photograph was taken from the new down platform of 1901 looking towards the impressive brush works buildings in the background. (A.W. Pinder/Author's collection)

Ivatt 'Atlantic' No. 278 approaching Wood Green station with a north-bound secondary, or 'stopping' train, the first portion consisting of four former six-wheeled carriages mounted on five, four-wheeled bogies. Making more fuss on the adjacent slow line with its suburban train is an Ivatt 0-6-2T. (Author's collection)

vehicles, two were stripped of their wheels and mounted together on three, four-wheeled bogies and put into service at the start of 1907. Between then and the First World War, nearly one hundred articulated 'twin' sets were created as well as sets of three carriages carried on four bogies, and four carriages carried on five bogies. The articulation principle was also perpetuated when new stock was built for London suburban services at the end of Gresley's term as Carriage & Wagon Superintendent.

Commuter traffic

By the turn of the new century, electric motors had proved a reliable form of traction on the new 'tube' underground lines in London, and this encouraged the GNR to approach a number of companies in 1903 to supply it with plans and costings for electrification of the main line between King's Cross and New Barnet as well as the High Barnet, Edgware, Enfield and Alexandra Palace branches. Estimates of the potential income to be derived, however, did not appear to cover the initial expenditure and agreement would have had to be reached with the SE&CR and NLR which ran over the same routes. Consequently, the GNR decided not to proceed with electrification and presented Ivatt with the challenge of designing a steam locomotive with acceleration to match that of underground electric trains. At first eleven tank versions of his 0-8-0 locomotive – with the addition of a pair of trailing wheels under the coal bunker – were employed between 1904 and 1907. The London based 0-8-2Ts were soon replaced by tank engines with a 0-6-2 wheel arrangement, capable of the same and necessary rapid acceleration but better

At the end of July 1907 the SE&CR passenger services between Victoria and GNR suburban stations, sometimes as far as New Barnet via King's Cross were withdrawn. Consisting of four-wheeled stock, one of those last services is seen at Belle Isle, between Maiden Lane or Gas Works and Copenhagen tunnels, with part of King's Cross goods yard just visible in the background.
(F. Moore's Photographs/ Author's collection)

Ivatt 0-8-2T No. 139 built in 1906 photographed at Colwick with an engineering train including travelling crane. (F. Moore's Photographs – Locomotive Publishing Co. 2707/ Author's collection)

suited to the awkward connections with the MetR at King's Cross. Between 1907 and 1912, fifty-six of these engines were completed at Doncaster all but four that went to the West Riding employed in and around London. The displaced 0-8-2Ts were re-allocated to Colwick and lines in the West Riding. The 0-6-2Ts proved very capable machines and Gresley produced a version with a larger boiler, sixty being built between the end of 1920 and the spring of the following year.

The Grantham accident of 1906

The Edwardian period in railway history was tainted by a number of serious accidents. Three of these were high-speed derailments: on the London & South Western Railway at Salisbury, 1 July 1906; on the GNR at Grantham, 19 September 1906; and on the LNWR at Shrewsbury, 15 October 1907. Of those three, Grantham has never been satisfactorily explained.

The indisputable facts are that the down 8.45pm mail train from King's Cross with sleeping carriages for Scotland ran through Grantham station where it should have stopped at 11pm. The junction at the north end of the station was set for the Nottingham branch, and although the engine managed to stay on the rails through the reverse curves, the tender was derailed. It pulled the engine onto its side before plunging down the embankment with a number of carriages. The vans that had been immediately behind the tender ran into the engine and caught fire and another fire broke out

amongst the wreckage at the bottom of the embankment. Driver F.W. Fleetwood and his fireman, Doncaster premium apprentice R. Talbot, were killed, along with nine passengers and a Post Office mail van attendant. Nineteen others were injured, two later dying of their injuries.

Local and national newspapers were soon full of speculation as to the causes of the crash. The local coroner's court took evidence and more opinions than facts were expressed there. Then five days after the accident, the official Board of Trade enquiry was opened and that lasted three days. Ivatt reported on the condition of the engine after he had examined it, and two staff involved with the train during its stop at Peterborough gave statements about the operation of the brakes. Their evidence supported the view that the engine was in sound mechanical condition and that the brakes were in working order. Attention then focused on the scene of the accident and the footplate crew. Post Office and GNR staff on the station the night of the accident gave statements, and testimonies were taken from drivers and firemen who had either worked with or had known Fleetwood or Talbot, with the intention of trying to ascertain whether either of these two men could have failed in their duties. Much of the conclusion in the Board of Trade Report was concerned with the characters of Fleetwood and Talbot and their working relationship. Fleetwood had recently had time off work because of illness and might have become ill on the night of the accident. There were

Grantham station as it appeared at the time of the 1906 accident, 'Atlantic' No. 1423 of 1907 slowing its train ready to stop alongside the down platform, unlike No. 276 that failed to do so on the night of 19 September. In the branch line platform, relegated from main line duties, is Grantham shed's 4-2-2 No. 268 with a train to either Nottingham or Lincoln. (E. Pouteau/Author's collection)

The Ivatt 'Atlantic' No. 276 involved in the Grantham accident of 1906 photographed leaving Doncaster for the south, either shortly before or after that unfortunate event. (Author's collection)

Very quickly after the Grantham accident, a series of postcards were produced, this example being one of the better copies that have survived. The ECJS bogie carriages with their distinctive clerestory roofs make a sad sight. (Commercial postcard/Author's collection)

unsubstantiated reports of him drinking, and there was even a suggestion his fireman might have been trying to wrestle control of the engine from him as they passed through the station. There was no evidence for any of these scenarios.

In the conclusion to his Board of Trade Report, Lt. Col. P.G. von Donop, RE,

A view looking north across Harlaxton Road, Grantham, crowded with spectators. The carriage nearest the signal bracket and overhanging Old Wharf Road is ECJS composite brake van No. 347, a vehicle carried on two, six-wheel bogies, and built as one of a batch of ten at Doncaster in 1903. (Commercial postcard/Author's collection)

The south end of Peterborough station taken about the time of the Grantham accident and showing Ivatt 'Atlantic' No. 280 of 1904 leaving with a train for King's Cross. On the extreme left, a six-wheeled carriage and van are parked in the short siding that may have housed the van that was attached to the rear of Fleetwood's train on 19 September 1906. (J.B. Sherlock/Author's collection)

after summarising the evidence, making suggestions and then dismissing them, could only state with certainty that the train was derailed because it was travelling too fast through the junction. He '…feared, therefore, that the primary cause of this accident must for ever remain a mystery.'

Seventy-five years after the accident another explanation was put forward by an ex-GNR employee and one time Station Inspector at Grantham. He believed the vacuum brake pipe between the tender of the engine and the first van might not have been attached by the shunter at Peterborough where Fleetwood's 'Atlantic' took over from the King's Cross engine. If the locomotive's pipe remained on its plug on the tender and, as he believed, the brakes on the train had been released to facilitate a speedier change over at Peterborough, then Fleetwood would have been able to pull away with an unbraked train. As the train would have been climbing almost all the way to Grantham, the driver would only have realised the train brakes were inoperative on the approach to the station, too late for the engine's brakes alone to be sufficient to slow its progress. After so many years since the accident, there is no way of substantiating these claims. No matter how convinced of his theory the ex-GNR employee was, the cause of the accident must remain unexplained.

The final years before World catastrophe

When HRH King George V assumed the throne in 1911, British society was very different from what it had been only ten years previously. For the first time, working

The state of progress on a new road bridge to replace the level crossing at the north end of Doncaster station on 17 June 1909. The photographer was facing almost directly along the centre line of the future bridge. The two brick structures either side of the railway tracks covered the subway beneath the railway. (Author's collection)

Looking from almost the same spot as the previous photograph when the Doncaster bridge had been completed. It was officially opened on 12 May 1910. Visible on the left is Frenchgate Junction signalbox, another of the many new signalboxes brought into use in the early 1870s. (Commercial postcard/Author's collection)

A detail from another Edwardian photograph that was turned into a commercial postcard, this one showing Crescent Bridge, Peterborough having the finishing touches put to it before its opening in April 1913. The contractor's name – The Cleveland Bridge & Engineering Co. Ltd., Darlington – is prominently displayed on the roof of the shed. (Commercial postcard/Author's collection)

A spirited start with a King's Cross-bound express from Peterborough, captured on film by the aptly named The Rapid Photograph Co. of Peterborough. 'Atlantic' No. 1439 is passing under the new Crescent Bridge and approaching the site of the closed Marsh Road level crossing it superseded. (Commercial postcard/Author's collection)

people had the assurance of a state-paid old age pension as well as limited unemployment and health insurance. Trades Unions had become stronger and railway workers were prepared to strike for better pay and conditions (as they did in 1911) without the fear of dismissal. Women were prepared to fight to be enfranchised. The idea of a 'better life in the countryside' was becoming a reality for many middle class families moving out of London to what later became 'Metro-Land', the new suburban developments along the MetR out of the city. The New Town movement was also seeing the tangible results of its

campaigning as the first newly planned settlement at Letchworth took shape. In May 1913, the GNR opened a generous new station there to replace its temporary two platforms.

The Shops Act of 1911 had introduced half-day closing, giving workers more leisure time, and by then annual summer holidays were enjoyed by both middle class and working class people alike. Skegness had become such a popular destination for East Midlanders that having absorbed the Wainfleet & Firsby Railway in July 1896, the GNR had set about doubling the line to the coast,

A little crowd of Edwardian men and one, slightly surprised, young woman, stand on the main departure platform at King's Cross station as the clock shows 11.18am. The departure roll indicates the next train is the 11.45am either stopping at, or with through carriages, or providing connections to Hatfield, Hitchin, Cambridge, Peterborough, Boston, Grimsby, Grantham, Newark, Retford, Sheffield, Manchester, Liverpool, Doncaster, Selby, Hull and York. (Commercial postcard – Bell's Photographic Co. Leigh-on-Sea/Author's collection)

A country gent and his two sons? Whoever they were, they were travelling south from Tuxford in the first years of the twentieth century, their appearance as well groomed as the station and its environs. (Detail from Commercial postcard/ Author's collection)

An Edwardian photograph of Hitchin station showing the recently rebuilt canopy and down platform buildings including a subway that replaced the footbridge. (WHS Kingsway Real Photo Series postcard/Author's collection)

completing that work and the enlargement of Skegness station by June 1900. Day trips from London started in the summer of 1905, and from 1908 were promoted with the help of the soon to be famous 'Jolly Fisherman' poster. In 1913, a new line between Conningsby Junction on the 'Loop' line and Bellwater Junction on the East Lincolnshire Line was brought into use that allowed holiday trains to run directly from the north through Lincoln to Skegness and Mablethorpe without having to reverse at Boston.

Coinciding with the new Georgian age was the appointment of a new GNR Locomotive Engineer. Having changed the appearance of the company's coaching stock, when Gresley took charge of the Locomotive Department in 1911 he was poised to modernise the GNR's motive power as well. At the time management was focused on improving the operation of goods and mineral traffic, bringing Control Offices into use first at Leeds Central in 1912 and then Nottingham London Road Low Level station in the summer of the following year, and later at King's Cross, Lincoln and Doncaster. Consequently, Gresley's first new design of locomotive after he had turned out a series of modified Ivatt 0-6-0s, was a 'mixed traffic' engine that could be used for both passenger and freight work. It had the same 2-6-0 wheel

arrangement first seen on the GNR at the turn of the century in the form of the maligned 'Yankees'. Although the boiler diameter was a modest 4ft 8in (1.42m), the same as Ivatt's original series of 'Atlantics', it was pressed to 170psi and was fitted with a superheater. The engine was visually distinctive by having Walschaerts valve gear, not as an experiment as it was on Ivatt's 'Klondyke' or compounds, but obviously intended to be another new standard feature. The locomotive appeared from Doncaster Works in August 1912 and was followed by nine more turned out between February and April the following year. It was a careful start, as though the new boy was deliberately being modest, even though his aspirations were much bolder. That was confirmed at the end of that year when three much larger freight engines were turned out from Doncaster Works. The wheel arrangement of these locomotives was 2-8-0 and the boilers were 5ft 6in (1.67m) in diameter making them the largest engines yet built for the GNR. Two more followed in January and March 1914, and then between April and June that year another batch of 2-6-0s appeared also fitted with 5ft 6in (1.67m) boilers. Gresley obviously had plans for a new express passenger locomotive at this time, but these had to be postponed when Britain declared war on Germany only two months later.

The new platform buildings and footbridge at Corby Glen station, one of those rebuilt as the up and down slow lines were extended northwards from Tallington to Stoke Summit in 1912/3. (Author's collection)

Standing at the south end of Nottingham Victoria station, it is uncertain how far Ivatt 4-4-0 No. 1317 would have taken the pre-First World War holiday makers because, apart from Skegness, all the other destinations listed on the headboard were reached over the tracks of the M&GN Joint. (Author's collection)

2-6-0 No. 1639 completed in 1913, was the last of a batch of ten of Gresley's first entirely new design for the GNR as its last Locomotive Engineer. The train is travelling south and approaching Wood Green station. (Gordon Tidey/Author's collection)

THE FIRST WORLD WAR AND THE AFTERMATH

It could be argued Doncaster Works was well prepared for the demands put upon it during the war because over the previous twenty years it had been considerably modernised. Wagon building had been removed to separate accommodation on the Carrs in 1889, with carriage building remaining part of the main site, where in 1897 a new 'West Carriage Shop' was erected. A new Locomotive Erecting Shop had been built in 1891/2, and to concentrate the repair of engines and improve the efficiency of that process, the impressive Crimpsall Repair Shop was constructed between 1899 and 1901 with a capacity of 100 engines.

A postcard of Huntingdon station posted on 29 January 1914 when a world war was furthest from anyone's thoughts. The morning sun is shining and the hanging baskets of flowers catch the light coming through the glass in the up platform canopy. On the town's memorial there will be 118 names of local men who were killed in the First World War. (WHS Kingsway Real Photo Series/Author's collection)

The interior of Crimpsall Repair Shop, Doncaster, with Ivatt 4-4-0 No. 1345 of 1898 slung from a pair of thirty-five ton overhead, travelling cranes proudly carrying cast-iron plates with their makers name – Craven Brothers Ltd, Manchester – and the dates, 1900 and 1901. (Great Northern Railway Society/p102665)

A new Tender Shop and large new Paint Shop erected at the same time were all part of this major renewal at the 'Plant'. Consequently, Doncaster was able to make a major contribution to the war effort by producing among many items horse-drawn Army vehicles, parts for field guns, nearly 125,000 six-inch high explosive shells, almost 4,300,000 cartridge cases for 18-pounder guns, and 20,000 artillery wheel spokes.

Out on the network, under Government control through the Railway Executive Committee, the movement of goods and HM Forces personnel took priority over ordinary passenger traffic. Although no speed restrictions were introduced, schedules were cut and services combined, resulting in long, heavy trains, while the myriad of through carriages almost disappeared. Trains took men to the ports for transhipment to fight in Europe and elsewhere, while as many trains brought them back either dead or wounded to grieving families. It was all too chillingly efficient, as though human cargoes had simply replaced the peacetime trains of potatoes and other vegetables. And in the potato fields of Lincolnshire, plans were drawn up on how the GNR's lines there might be used in the event of invasion. The vast Army camp at Belton, just north-east

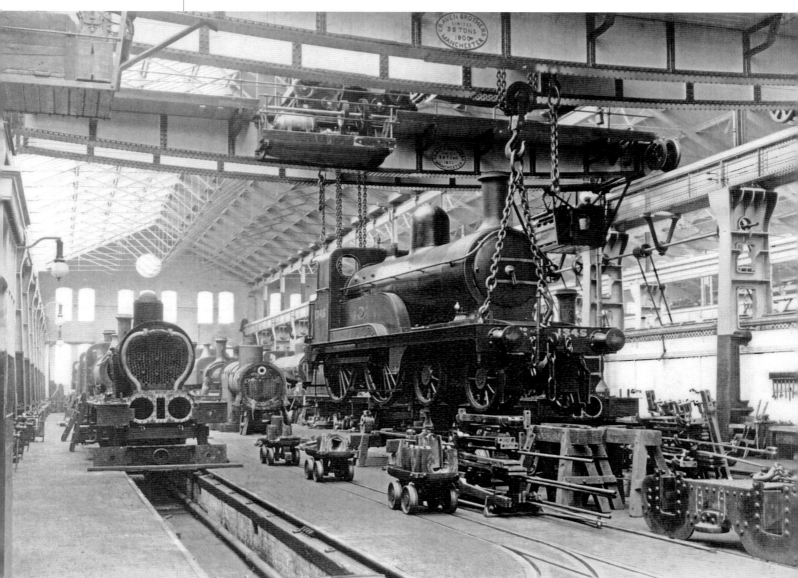

A postcard sized photograph with 'to Sergt Mackie with compliments Cpt Conley France 7.7.18' written on the back. Still in GNR livery but with the letters 'R O D' applied to the tender, 0-6-0 No. 394 posed for its portrait at Wizernes station in north-west France. (Author's collection)

Ivatt 4-2-2 No. 265 pulling away from Boston at the end of its short working life. The twelve engines of this class were withdrawn at the same time in December 1917. No. 265 was stored at its last home shed at Peterborough before being scrapped at Doncaster the following year. (P.W. Pilcher FB3147/ Author's collection)

One of a number of posed photographs showing women employed by the railways during the First World War. Five cleaners are working on a couple of the GNR's six-wheel coaches. (Author's collection)

The Royal train passing South Yorkshire Junction, Doncaster, and heading south in 1916 as though nothing was amiss with the world. In reality, the war appeared to have no end, Russia was on the point of revolution and within two years HRH King George V's first cousins would lose their positions as heads of Germany and Russia. (Regina Co. Press Photographers, Doncaster postcard/Author's collection)

In 1917, the GNR took on Miss Nun as 'telegraph lad' at Hitchin Yard box, where she is seen at the bank of single needle telegraph instruments. Despite its name, the box was an important location on the main line and the role of 'telegraph lad' was not a nominal appointment but an important position, especially with war-time traffic being so heavy. (Author's collection)

Gresley's first batch of 0-6-2Ts were built in 1920, and No. 1727 seen here was only a few months old when photographed piloting Ivatt 'Atlantic' No. 1428 out of the London terminus with the 9.50am relief 'Flying Scotsman'. Congreve bridge at this location had just been removed but Battlebridge Road bridge is still prominent in the background. (Gordon Tidey/Author's collection)

of Grantham, was connected to the GNR main line by a four and a half mile (7.2km) long branch.

In 1916 and 1917, twenty-six 0-6-0s were modified with condensing equipment and sent to France. With these gone and older locomotives continuing to work when they were due for retirement, it was still necessary for Doncaster to build new engines, and in 1916 ten more 2-6-0s were constructed along with ten more of Gresley's new 0-6-0 tank engine design.

Late in 1916 many stations all over the country were closed to save money (and men) and track taken up ostensibly for use 'abroad'. At Cranwell in Lincolnshire the Royal Naval Air Service brought into use a new airfield, the camp there connected to the GNR's Sleaford–Barkston East line. (After the war, Cranwell became the site of the RAF's officer training college.) In 1917 a standard timetable for all goods and mineral trains running between Peterborough and London was introduced. Soon 500-ton passenger trains were being worked out of King's Cross, requiring double-heading at least as far as Potters Bar.

Finally in November 1918 the armed conflict was brought to an official end, having cost the lives of 980 GNR men of the 10,038 employees that had joined HM Forces.

Another 'loop' line

Before looking at the post-war years leading up to the Grouping of Britain's railways in 1923, the GNR's last major addition to its network needs to be chronicled.

As mentioned previously, in the 1880s discussions had once again turned to the creation of a 'loop' line to ease pressure on the main line on the approaches to the capital. The decision then had been to lay additional tracks and provide extra tunnels on the existing main line between King's Cross and New Barnet. New up and down slow lines were laid north of Potters Bar, through Hatfield to just south of Digswell viaduct, four tracks starting again just north of Welwyn North tunnel from Woolmer Green through Knebworth and Stevenage to Hitchin. The creation of much

of this latter section had been achieved right at the end of the century. But the provision of additional tunnels at Hadley Wood, Potters Bar and Welwyn as well as the widening of Digswell Viaduct had been resisted on the grounds of cost. In 1894 the Board had sought prices for this work and predictably considered the expenditure could not be justified. Once again it turned to ideas for a 'relief line'. The preferred plan was for a new line northwards from Enfield, then the terminus of the branch leaving the main line at Wood Green, to Langley 2.5miles (4km) south of Stevenage where it would link up again with the main line. Although more expensive than any widening scheme, the added attraction of this new route was that it had the potential to create new revenue streams by opening up new areas for development. The Board supported this view and the Act for the new line was secured in 1898.

It took another twenty-five years before the line was completed. Changes of route were made requiring another Act, yet another Act for an extension of time to complete the project had to be secured and it was not until January 1906 that the first construction contract was let. That was only for the section from Enfield to Cuffley that opened in April 1910 (in good time to transport people to see the remains of the Zeppelin shot down there in September 1916). The next contract was let in July 1912 for the extension from Cuffley to Hertford, and then following the third Act for an extension of time secured in 1914 work was finally put in hand to reach Langley Junction. The difficulties of acquiring materials and construction workers slowed work throughout the war years and it was not until March 1918 that goods trains were able to transverse the whole route. Even then they were only able to use a single track between Cuffley and Langley Junction, and Tyer's specialist 'Absolute–Permissive' token instruments had to be installed to regulate their movement. Completion of double-track was not achieved until after the GNR had been absorbed into the LNER, a passenger service starting in June 1924.

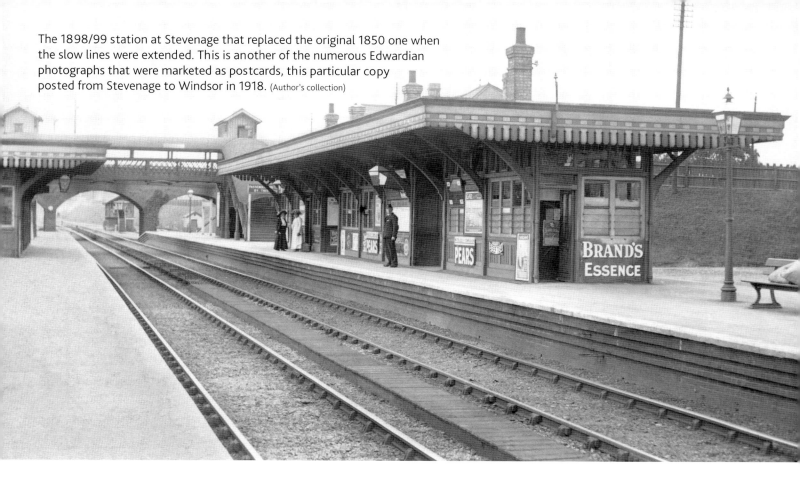

The 1898/99 station at Stevenage that replaced the original 1850 one when the slow lines were extended. This is another of the numerous Edwardian photographs that were marketed as postcards, this particular copy posted from Stevenage to Windsor in 1918. (Author's collection)

Rendlesham Viaduct under construction, one of two such structures on the GNR's extension between Enfield and Cuffley that opened in 1910. Rendlesham Viaduct was 495ft (151m) long, consisted of fourteen arches and was 66ft (20m) at its highest point. (F. Moore Railway Photographs/Author's collection)

The GNR's last years

The First World War marked the end of Britain's great railway age. Change had been evident before the war, but what was lost in the years between 1914 and 1918 was the spirit of enterprise. The country's railways had been required to cope with changed priorities, and after 1918 and through into the 1920s, the feeling continued that they were simply just coping with traffic. In the summer of 1914 the GNR's fastest service from London to Bradford had been 3hr 56min; at the end of the war it was 4hr 50min. Between London and Leeds in either direction the fastest pre-war train had taken 3hr 25min compared to 4hr 10min in 1918. A traveller in 1914 could complete the journey from King's Cross to Edinburgh by East Coast Joint service in 7hr 45min; at the end of 1918 the same trip occupied five minutes short of an additional two hours. Services did recover after 1918 but not to the same pre-war levels. Train travel became ordinary. If the public wanted to be thrilled by speed then they no longer looked to the railways as they had done during the 'races' of the late Victorian age. They turned instead to the feats of individual racers such as Louis Rigolly who, in 1904, had been the first man to drive a car faster than 100mph (103mph). In 1920, an authenticated 156mph was achieved at Daytona, USA and in that same year, in the air, Joseph Sadi-Lecointe flew his plane at 171mph. Only three years later he was able to attain 232mph.

Before and during the War, Gresley had continued to fit engines with superheaters, but he had also begun to

A pre-war scene showing all the bustle of the Edwardian capital city around King's Cross station. This photograph, like so many others, was turned into a postcard, this one posted from Finsbury Park to Barnsley in November 1921. (Rotary Photo, London postcard/Author's collection)

The last of the pre-war batch of five Gresley two-cylinder 2-8-0s, No. 460, passing northwards through New Southgate station on the down slow line. As was the practice at the time, any cattle wagons that needed to be in a train were marshalled next to the engine, the lime used to clean and sterilise them making the five in this goods train particularly noticeable. (Gordon Tidey/Author's collection)

The end of the war did not bring peace in Britain's labour relations and in 1920 there was a strike of coal miners, followed by a more prolonged walk-out between April and June 1921. To save coal, a number of GNR locomotives were modified to burn oil. One of those was 2-6-0 No. 1667, photographed on the southern approaches to Oakleigh Park station overtaking NLR 4-4-0 on a suburban train from Broad Street to Potters Bar. (Author's collection)

Since Sturrock's time, GNR Locomotive Engineers had rebuilt engines they had inherited in order to try and improve their efficiency and performance. In 1912/3, Gresley fitted new boilers to six Ivatt 4-4-0s, and No. 1317 seen here at Gedling was one of those engines. (F.H. Gillford/Author's collection)

The last batch of Ivatt 4-4-0s built in 1911 were all equipped with superheaters from new, and No. 56 of that series is seen heading north with a late afternoon 'stopping passenger' train at the south end of Wood Green station c.1921. (Gordon Tidey/Author's collection)

Outside King's Cross 'Top Shed', Gresley's Wolseley is sandwiched between Stirling's preserved pioneer '8ft single' No. 1 and Ivatt's 'Atlantic' experimentally rebuilt with four cylinders in 1915. (Author's collection)

consider multi-cylinder engines. In 1915 large boiler 'Atlantic' No. 279 had been rebuilt with four cylinders as a precursor to the construction of a larger engine with most probably a 4-6-2 'Pacific' wheel arrangement. Following trials with the 'Atlantic' that showed no real improvement in performance, ideas turned to three cylinder propulsion, and in 1916 a 2-8-0 was built at Doncaster with Walschaerts gear on the two outside cylinders and Gresley's own design of gear to activate the valves of the inside cylinder. Following discussions in 1919 with H. Holcroft of the South Eastern & Chatham Railway (SECR), who had patented a form of gear for three cylinder engines, Gresley re-designed his arrangement. This was then fitted to another locomotive, that like the appearance of Ivatt's pioneer large boilered 'Atlantic' in 1902, caused quite a stir when it was put to work in March 1920. It was a three cylinder 2-6-0 with a six foot (1.83m) diameter boiler that made Ivatt's 'Atlantic' look small. The huge vessel was also pressed to 180psi. Nine more of these engines were built between then and the summer of 1921. The same cylinder and valve gear arrangement was then incorporated into a new 2-8-0 locomotive design, the North British Locomotive Co. being entrusted with constructing a batch of ten in 1921.

Gresley's large-boilered 2-6-0s showed their worth during the coal strike of 1921. Many services were combined and former railwayman and writer, W.A. Tuplin in his book, *Great Northern Steam* (Ian Allan, 1971), vividly recalled a journey as the driver of one of this class between Doncaster and King's Cross in that year when three trains had been combined to give a total of nineteen bogie carriages. A similar long south-bound train is seen here passing through Wood Green station. (Gordon Tidey/Author's collection)

At Greenwood, just north of New Barnet, 2-6-0 No. 1003 appears to be making light work of a fully fitted down goods during the coal strike of 1921; certainly the fireman seems content to hang out the cab. The lofty GNR signals would be replaced by somersaults on shorter, reinforced concrete, posts within two years. (Gordon Tidey/Author's collection)

Hauled by an unidentified 2-6-0, a southbound train threads its way through the extensive Decoy sidings at The Carrs, Doncaster during the 1921 strike year. (Author's collection)

A detail of another Gordon Tidey photograph taken during the summer of 1921, and included, not only because it is a beautiful locomotive portrait, but also to show New Southgate No. 2 signalbox, tucked in under one of the arches of Friern Barnet Road bridge and requiring a most impressive flue from the stove. (Gordon Tidey/Author's collection)

Gresley's three cylinder 2-8-0 No. 485 was the penultimate of a batch of ten of this design built for the GNR by the North British Locomotive Works of Glasgow in 1921. It is making its way along the up slow line past Farrows factory at Peterborough. The down slow line had yet to reach this location when the photograph was taken but would occupy the site of the grassy bank in the foreground. (Author's collection)

A view from Friern Barnet Road bridge, New Southgate, as brand new Gresley 0-6-2 suburban tank No. 1736, completed at Doncaster Works in 1921, rushes through with a north-bound outer suburban train of new Gresley articulated stock. The camera's shutter speed was not sufficient to 'freeze' the action, but the image gives a wonderful impression of these smartly timed services. (Author's collection)

Gresley's pioneer 4-6-2 'Pacific', No. 1470 *Great Northern*, heading north at Wood Green shortly after completion at Doncaster Works in April 1922. The length of the train does not appear to be more than eleven carriages, so this could be considered a modest load in contrast to the 500–600 ton trains of the previous coal strike year. (Gordon Tidey/Author's collection)

Then in April 1922 the predicted 'Pacific' made its appearance from Doncaster Works. The interruption of war, when new developments were put on hold, had allowed a longer and more useful gestation period for this locomotive. Outline drawings survive of earlier manifestations, the first having the appearance of an elongated Ivatt 'Atlantic' with the four cylinder arrangement Gresley had tried on No. 279. The three-cylinder 'Pacific' was a new, beautifully proportioned and very obviously modern engine, the boiler of a carefully thought out tapered design, the two outside cylinders with Walschaerts valve gear having the piston rods supported on the same neat three-bar crosshead and slide bars as on the 2-6-0 and, hidden out of sight, Gresley's mechanism for the middle cylinder. With the 'Grouping' of the country's railways only a few months away, the engine was christened *Great Northern* and its anonymous sibling that was completed a little later, was soon named *Sir Frederick Banbury*, after the GNR's last Chairman. The performance and later development of this design is not for this narrative, but again it has to be said that although the engine and those derived from it gained a reputation for speed, its genesis was a response to the need for greater haulage power to eliminate the double-heading of trains out of King's Cross mentioned above. As if to emphasis this, in early September 1922, twenty carriages making up a 610-ton train were coupled behind *Sir Frederick Banbury* at King's Cross to see just what Gresley's new design could pull. Not only did the engine have no trouble coping with the load, but speeds of over 70mph were recorded at a number of locations between Hitchin and Grantham.

The Grouping

Unlike in 1909, when the GNR, GCR and GER first proposed amalgamation but MPs were still wedded to the Victorian values of *laissez-faire* and competition, the war years had opened the Government's eyes to the advantages of a more co-ordinated and co-operative method of running the nation's railways. Nationalisation was considered but rejected and instead it decided to group most of the hundreds of private railways into four larger organisations to achieve 'economy of scale'. Of the four groups, the GNR was to be absorbed into the London & North Eastern Railway (LNER) along with the NER, GCR, GER, North British Railway (NBR) and the Great North of Scotland Railway.

Despite the inevitability of the Grouping, the GNR did not free-wheel through its last years as an independent company. Gresley's new locomotives were probably the most obvious signs of progress. But there were indications of change in other areas as well. Shortly after A.E. Tattersall was appointed as the company's Signal Superintendent in June 1920 he introduced a few American three-position upper quadrant semaphores at King's Cross and Belle Isle. The progressive ideas outlined in his 1921 book *Modern Developments in Railway Signalling* may well have transformed GNR signalling practice still further had he not been given at first a subordinate position with the new LNER and then promoted in 1928 to the North Eastern Area of the company. Here he did make considerable changes that laid the foundations for later twentieth and early twenty-first century British signalling.

The GNR also had three significant major civil engineering projects in hand as the Grouping came into effect. New slow lines were being laid between Offord & Buckden and Huntingdon stations, necessitating the construction of another double-track viaduct over the River Ouse and the widening of a long embankment. This section was brought into use at the beginning of 1925. Quadruple track continued northwards from Huntingdon through Abbotts Ripton to Connington. Although double track remained over Conington Fen and through Holme station to Yaxley, three miles (4.8km) south of Peterborough, additional up and down slow lines from there to Crescent Junction Peterborough were also completed shortly after the Grouping. As part of this work, substantial double-track steel bridges were erected over the River Nene immediately south of the station, making a stark contrast to the cast-iron spans of the original 1850 viaduct at this location.

The third piece of work was undoubtedly the most obvious to the ordinary traveller as it completely transformed the appearance in a very familiar GNR location. For many years there had been two over-bridges between the end of the main line platforms and Maiden Lane or Gas Works tunnels at King's Cross. The one closest to the tunnel mouths took Congreve Street over York Road station to the Imperial Gas Works on the western side of the main station site. The other bridge nearest the main station took Battle Bridge Road across the tracks. Whereas Congreve Street bridge had been there since at least the early 1860s, the Battle Bridge one had appeared some time in the 1880s or early 1890s. After the gas works was moved to a new site in 1911, Congreve Street bridge was removed, but it was not until 1921/22 that Battle Bridge bridge came down as part of the excavation of the former gas works land to make way for new locomotive facilities. These were completed just after the Grouping, in time for the introduction of the fleet of Gresley 'Pacifics'.

At the Grouping the LNER inherited from the GNR just under 900 tender locomotives, nearly 500 tank engines, approximately 3,500 carriages and just over 38,000 goods vehicles of all descriptions, although the majority were open wagons. The number of locomotives made up just over 18 per cent of the LNER's total, about the same percentage as bequeathed by the GCR and GER (29 per cent coming from the NER and just over 14 per cent from the NBR). More significantly, the new company inherited H.N. Gresley as its Chief Mechanical Engineer, with a staff that included many men who would go on to high office over the following decades. It was along the GNR main line that the most prestigious of the LNER's expresses were to run, culminating in the streamlined services of the late 1930s whilst the GCR main line gently slumbered. And of course, it was a locomotive – *Mallard* – whose pedigree could be traced back to the 1921 'Pacific', *Great Northern*, that captured, and still retains, the world speed record for a steam locomotive.

With the Grouping only a few months away, Ivatt 'Atlantic' No. 1445 is seen leaving King's Cross and passing the substantial retaining wall of the adjacent gas works. This and the building that appears above the cab and tender of the engine would soon be demolished and the land behind brought down to track level to provide space for a locomotive stabling and servicing area. (Gordon Tidey/Author's collection)

A little crowd admire the GNR's new locomotive on a grey day at King's Cross in 1922. Gresley's *Great Northern* was certainly a fitting end to the independent life of the company whose name it bore as well as a fitting beginning to the life of the London & North Eastern Railway (LNER) the following year. (Author's collection)

PEOPLE

Something of the spirit of the age of the Stirling '8ft single' is captured in this photograph. Working conditions were hard and discipline strict but the driver here is demonstrating that both he and his machine are on top of the job, and his chosen perch hints at a certain bravado. (Author's collection)

On the right is the same driver that had sat above the driving wheel of Stirling '8ft single' No. 53. Sadly he remains anonymous; he and his fireman are posed in front of Stirling 2-2-2 No. 230, turned out from Doncaster Works in April 1887. (F. Moore's Photographs – detail/ Author's collection)

Different locomotive, different driver but the same fireman as was photographed in front of 2-2-2 No. 230. This time the locomotive was No. 873, one of the last Stirling 2-2-2s and completed at Doncaster Works in March 1892. When the engine was withdrawn in 1911, drivers could be earning between 5s (25p) and 7s (35p) per day, depending on their years of service. (F. Moore's Photographs – Locomotive Publishing Co. 1315 – detail/ Author's collection)

The most notable aspect of this photograph is not the new down line, riveted steel bridge shortly after it had been moved into position over the Trent Dyke north of Newark on 16 September 1889, nor the benevolent expression of George Clay, Inspector of Works, Doncaster as he poses proudly for his portrait, but the fact that someone had brought a domestic kitchen chair for old George to sit on! (Author's collection)

At the end of the nineteenth century photographs were taken of bridges all over the GNR network as an official record of their condition. This is a detail of the photograph taken to record the road bridge over the railway at Nutbrook on the Heanor branch, but the photographer was also happy to allow the staff shunting there at the time to pose whilst he took the shot. It was obviously a good working day, as all three men are trying hard not to smile too much. The 0-6-0 No. 1042 was brand new at the time, built for the GNR by Dubs & Co. of Polmadie, Glasgow in 1896. (Author's collection)

Although not the intention of the photographer, this shot could almost have been one of those 'what not to do' educational images, because to support himself on the walkway, the figure is grasping both the down rods operating the home and distant signals. He has yet to place the signal lamps of those two signals in position, having already mounted the lamp complete with its outer case behind the spectacle of the 'splitting distant' on the left. This particular bracket of somersaults was just south of Huntingdon station before quadruple track was brought into use in 1924/5.
(Author's print from glass plate negative formerly in Ian Allan Library)

Pipers Wood on the main line between Bawtry and Rossington. The photograph was taken to record the work of excavating the trench to take the new 15in (38.2cm) water main from Bawtry to Doncaster in the spring of 1902. The photographer and three men stand on the down main with the signal clear for the approach of a train. John Holland, standing on the rail, was killed by a light engine here on 6 March 1910.
(Peterborough Museum Ce3)

The inspector with his bowler hat and rolled umbrella, glances back at the photographer with a look of slight uneasiness as at least twenty-five men work on a siding at the north end of Doncaster station. Unfortunately, the photograph is undated, but it has to have been taken a few years before 1910, when the road bridge that replaced Marshgate level crossing would have been prominent in the background.
(Peterborough Museum Ce11)

This is a photograph, either of Doncaster Works premier apprentices about to embark on a trip, or an arranged guided tour of 'The Plant'. There certainly appears to be two separate groups judging by the different dress codes, with four men in casual jackets and straw boaters and the remaining six attired in their best suits with stiff high collars and ties. Notice the second man from the left wearing a black arm band and another carrying a camera. They are all lined up in front of Ivatt 4-4-0 No. 50 built at 'The Plant' in 1909.
(Author's collection)

Another detail of a larger image with a little secret. Ivatt's 'Klondyke' No. 983 built at Doncaster during 1900 was fairly new when it posed for this photograph. Everyone stood still apart from the tabby cat that chose the exact moment the camera's shutter was released to jump from next to the lamp onto the right buffer. (Stephenson Locomotive Society 1843)

Some of the shunting staff at Colwick Yard standing in front of Stirling designed but Ivatt built 0-6-0 saddle tank No. 1262, that having been turned out from Doncaster Works in 1902, spent all its GNR working life at the Nottinghamshire marshalling yard. Behind the engine is Shunters' Cabin North and in the distance on the left a glimpse of the erecting shop with its flag at half mast. (Author's collection)

A detail from a postcard sent by J.S. Gilby (singled out from the group by the cross) to his aunt in Stratford, London on 2 June 1913. The man at the front of the group with the metal rod has paused from his task of taking up the setts that formed Thorpe Road level crossing south of Peterborough station visible in the background, part of the underside of the bridge that replaced the crossing at the top of this view. (J.F. Searle, Werrington postcard/Author's collection)

It's cold up north! The red noses of the staff of this West Riding station show up even in a black and white photograph taken in the winter of 1909. Behind them the posters announce alterations to the timetable from 1 November as well as – despite the time of year – excursions to the seaside every Monday, Wednesday and Saturday. Cleethorpes is an understandable holiday destination but Grimsby Docks is a little more questionable. (Author's collection)

The lineside dispatch apparatus and delivery net near Huntingdon used in conjunction with Travelling Post Office vans. The same arrangement was repeated at Bawtry, Retford, Newark, St Neot's, Sandy, Biggleswade, Hitchin, Stevenage, Welwyn, Hatfield, and New Barnet, although there are few, if any photographs of the equipment at those locations. By the mid 1880s the GNR was earning just over £25,000 per annum from carrying Royal Mail.
(Locomotive Publishing Co./ Author's collection 4234)

The crew of Gresley's 2-6-0 No. 1001 of 1920. Comment is almost unnecessary. (Author's collection)

The staff of the GNR's station at Tuxford photographed shortly before the Grouping of 1923. At the time the station master was Charles Lawrence, who is fourth from the right. As well as the humans, two other essential employees of such country stations were the shunting horse and the cat. The man on the left is standing on the turntable onto which every wagon in and out of the goods shed at Tuxford had to be turned, as the structure had been built in 1852, inconveniently, at right angles to the main line. The cast-iron wheel stops were intended to prevent vehicles rolling out of the shed and onto the main line only a few feet to the right. (Author's collection)

The author's great grandfather, Arthur Thorpe, finished his railway career as resident crossing keeper at Oster Fen Lane crossing, Claypole. This photograph was taken shortly after the Grouping when nothing much had changed for many years at this remote Lincolnshire location on the GNR main line. (Author's collection)

INDEX

(numbers in **bold** refer to images and their captions)